FLIGHT INTO SANITY

A Memoir of Recovery

The world is a better place for those who

refuse to believe they cannot fly

Sara Orbeton

Flight Into Sanity: A Memoir of Recovery
by Sara Orbeton

Signalman Publishing 2012
www.signalmanpublishing.com
email: info@signalmanpublishing.com
Kissimmee, Florida

Front cover artwork by Wendy Stanley

Cover layout by Joel Ramnaraine

ISBN: 978-1-935991-39-7 (paperback)
           978-1-935991-40-3 (ebook)

Library of Congress Control Number: 2011943578

Signalman
Publishing

ACKNOWLEDGMENTS

There are people who not only helped me make this book possible, but (probably unknowingly) helped me along my life's path to reach this wonderful place in my life. I started writing this as a self-awareness exercise with the goal to figure out why my life seemed so disconnected. I did achieve that goal. I have also experienced tremendous mental and spiritual growth as a result of this exercise.

When this began evolving into a cohesive story, my kind friend Polly Bennell helped with the first editing process, and then encouraged me to go on to make it a publishable book. My lifelong friend Dick Forringer, who has just recently published two books of his own, also helped me to go ahead with this and provided me with new resources to make it possible. However, Dick figures into the story at a much deeper level, as you will see when you read the book.

I wish to acknowledge the following people (and other creatures) whom I consider my angels. They have helped me, or "carried" me, along the way on this journey I call my life: Dick F.; Freda F.; my daughter, Jenni; my sister Donna; George Jones; Dr. Evans; Barbara M.; Tiger the cat; Zeppie the cat; three raccoons; three loons; Terry C.; and others whose names I do not know.

* Note that the name Orbeton is not in any way connected with my biological family. Orbeton is my married name.

INTRODUCTION

This book is an actual account of my experiences growing up in a family fraught with tragic losses, alcoholism, mental illness, domestic violence, and pedophilia. It is also about my own journey through mental illness and alcoholism—and my ultimate recovery and journey into a new life. I could not have written this narrative until I had reached healing and peace, a place where I could look back at my life without re-experiencing all of the pain. These are my truths and my own individual processes. I do not promise that my process of recovery will work for anyone else. I have been to the edge of life and back more than once and as I reflect, I realize I could have taken easier roads. However, I want to leave you with a promise of hope. I believe that human beings have the ability to heal from unbelievable pain and suffering. However, this healing does not come easy. There is much hard work, possibly additional pain and suffering, and the re-experiencing of events. This healing cannot be achieved in a vacuum—you must have help, someone you trust. At times I felt very alone. I felt as if I were on a roller-coaster ride in the dark. But the journey was (and continues to be) also like climbing a mountain—and the best way to the other side is over the top.

I have come to believe that people and opportunities are placed in our paths, but it is up to us to look in the right direction when they appear. I missed many opportunities because I was either under the influence of alcohol or was looking in the wrong direction. I have since learned to seek help from professionals, from spiritual sources, and from people who have walked a similar path. Learning to trust, and figuring out whom to trust, was a trial-and-error process, but it was necessary for me to continue my journey.

In this book, I have shared my experiences, the details of which may be difficult for some people to read, in hopes that those of you who may be on a similar path can realize that, with work and help, there is hope for a better life. I would also like to think that social workers, nurses, therapists, counselors, doctors, and others in the helping and health-care professions will gain insight about the importance of the time required to take these steps. Each person has his/her own unique story and his/her unique process of recovery. I believe that people can change for the better—if they are willing. People who have suffered mental, spiritual, and physical injuries caused by severe childhood trauma do not have to spend their lives believing they are "damaged goods." They can find healing and peace.

I have changed some of the names of some people in this story to protect their privacy. Those people whose actual names appear have given me permission to print them. The events in this book are true to the extent that I can remember them. I have shared this manuscript with other members of my family and they concur with my accounts of events and situations.

> "The world breaks everyone,
>
> and afterward, some are strong
>
> at the broken places."
>
> —Ernest Hemingway

TABLE OF CONTENTS

CHAPTER 1

the beginning of the end

July 24, 1997—Portland, Maine

The setting sun cast a pink-orange blanket on the islands and boats as I walked along the beach. Though the air was beginning to cool, there was a warm glow over everything. I saw no other people on the beach—for most people, it was time to go home. However, I was just arriving—I had a different mission this evening. My car was parked in the lot at Kettle Cove and would likely be ticketed for having been left overnight. But it didn't matter. I wouldn't be returning to my car. Eventually, someone would find the notes left on the dashboard and figure things out. By then, my mission would be completed.

I walked more than a mile down the beach, over the rocks and past the public beach, and sat down in a little cave-like spot formed by the rocks. The daylight was almost gone now, and I could see a lone sailboat anchored in the safety of the cove by Richmond Island. The warm yellow light coming from the portholes gave me the impression that they were happy and contented. I wondered where they were from. They didn't even know I existed.

Leaning against the rocks, I closed my eyes, not noticing the sharp edges digging into my skin. Mentally, I was already somewhere else. I checked my pocket to be sure the razor blade was still there, wrapped in paper. My plan was to cut deep into the veins in my wrist and allow myself to bleed out into the sand. No mess for anyone to clean up. I had taken four aspirin so the blood wouldn't clot. At this point, I was so numb, I doubted I would feel any pain.

Pain. I had already had so much pain—the kind that stays in your gut and your heart, the kind of pain that makes you immobile and dysfunctional. The kind of pain that wakes you up in the morning and stays with you all day. They call it depression. All the therapy and all the work I had done, and now after all this—forty-nine years of life—the pain was still there. I knew there were people who loved me and would be hurt if I did this. My daughter would be devastated. I did not want to hurt her, but I could not find any other way out. I felt like I had failed at everything, despite how hard I had tried to succeed. The pain was searing, and I couldn't make it go away.

As I sat there waiting for the right moment to end it all, my life began to play back in my mind, as though it was a long-playing video featuring important, life-changing events. I closed my eyes and let the video run.

CHAPTER 2

my mother

June 1953—Los Alamitos, California

I am walking along beside my mother, with one hand on a stroller that is carrying my baby sister, Joyce. On the other side of the stroller is my sister Donna. I am five years old, Donna is three, and Joyce is eight months old. My name is Sara.

The sun is relentless, the sidewalk so hot you could fry an egg on it, and I have to squint to keep the sun out of my eyes. As a redheaded, freckled, blue-eyed girl, my skin and eyes are extremely sensitive to the sun. We don't have a car or a phone, so we're on our way to a phone booth to call my father, who had abandoned us and returned to his job in Ohio after a brief six weeks trying to find "just the right job" in California.

My mother, who is a nurse, has found a good job in a polio hospital. But my father's domineering; controlling nature wasn't going to allow her to be the breadwinner in the family. Oh no. His idea was to go back to the job he left behind in Ashtabula, Ohio, because he said he didn't like working with the "coloreds" in California. It has torn the family up, but he had his own priorities.

My parents have already spent every penny they had moving to California, spurred by a doctor's suggestion that such a change of climate would improve my mother's health. Now my mother is working every day, paying for child care and rent, and she is incredibly lonely. Standing outside the phone booth, I watch my mother's tears run down her face and drip off the telephone receiver as she begs my father to come back. I feel the tears welling up in my own eyes, and I'm getting a little scared. The conversation ends with my mother slamming the phone down and crying deep, gut-wrenching sobs as she turns the stroller around and heads back to our apartment. Although she tells me that everything will be alright, I know that it won't.

How do you console your mother when you're five years old and you don't even know what's wrong? I look at my sister Donna, whose big blue eyes are wide open, staring at me and silently asking the question *What's wrong?* I don't know the answer.

My parents met when my father returned from World War II, having escaped from a prison camp in Germany where he was held for a year and a half. He had some terrible experiences in the prison camps, and when he returned to Ohio he discovered his parents had cashed in his life insurance and sold his car, assuming he had been killed. His girlfriend, Thelma, had married someone else, and was now the mother of a three-year-old daughter. But Thelma introduced him to her friend Jeanne, who, after a whirlwind three-month romance, became his wife in a civil ceremony in West Virginia. Jeanne, my mother, had graduated from nursing school, and she gave up a good job to marry my father. I'll never understand why she did that.

It's a bright sunny morning, a few days after the tear-filled phone call, and I am awakened by the sound of someone banging on a window near where I have been sleeping. I look up to discover I have been sleeping on a couch, in a house I don't recognize. The woman banging on the window asks me to open the door. Reluctantly, I open the door and the woman comes in and sits down with me, explaining that my mother and my baby sister, Joyce, are in the hospital. Donna and I would have to be taken somewhere to stay until my father arrives.

I later learn that my mother attempted suicide by turning on the gas oven in our apartment. My sister Joyce was there with her. They were discovered by a neighbor who smelled gas, an ambulance was called and they were taken to the hospital. My mother was put in jail and I don't know who took care of Joyce. My sister Donna and I were sent to an orphanage, where I can still remember the smell of dried urine everywhere. Dressed in gray uniforms, we lined up in the hallway each morning to say "good morning" in unison to someone named Mrs. Johnson. I remember being incredibly lonely, always looking for my sister. They didn't let us stay together while we were there. I wondered where my mother was, and why we were in this place. I was so scared. I can remember having a really bad dream one of those nights. I can only remember bits of it—people yelling, me crying, and my mother not being around. It scared me so much that I had a difficult time sleeping after that.

My father, accompanied by his brother, my uncle Bob, arrived a couple of weeks later, and the six of us—my parents, my sisters, my uncle, and I—traveled back to Ohio in a hot car, called a Packard, that had uncomfortable wool seats. There was no air-conditioning in those days. We left most of our belongings behind. I only vaguely remember the trip, with my parents arguing in the front seat, and my uncle in the backseat, telling us stories trying to cheer us up. For some reason, I had to sit on my uncle's lap and throughout the trip he put his fingers inside my panties. It was really icky and I hated it, but he kept whispering to me that this was our little secret. I think something inside me snapped when that happened—my life would be forever changed. It seemed like a terribly long, hot trip, but somehow we made it back to Ashtabula, Ohio, our home of origin.

Initially, we rented a big house in a quiet neighborhood and I remember making friends and having fun in the back yard. But after a few months, we moved to another house – well, it wasn't even a house, but one of several abandoned World War II army barracks. Apparently they rented those places cheaply to poor people. There were other poor families living there, too. The place was army-green, cold, and drafty, with the only source of heat being an oil stove in the middle of the living room. I know my mother hated the place, because she and my dad argued about it all the time. Sometimes I hid behind the couch when they fought, listening to her cry and begging him to stop hitting her.

As a rebellious act, my mother painted the front door bright red.

My mother's health continued to deteriorate. One day, in May 1954, I remember standing outside in front of our barrack, looking up at my beautiful, tall mother, who was holding books under her arm. She was saying to me, "Now, Sara, I have to go to the hospital for an operation. I will be there for a few days. If I don't come home, since you are the oldest [I was six], you will have to take care of Daddy and your sisters. Do you understand?" Even though I had no idea what she was talking about, I nodded my head. I loved her so much, and all I could think about was that she might not come home.

I was then put on a train and sent to stay with my great-aunt Dot in Pittsburgh, whom everyone said was "crazy." I don't know where my sisters went. Apparently, my father couldn't take care of us for a few days on his own. The next night, while my aunt was putting my hair up in pin curls, the phone rang. My aunt answered it and began crying great, bellowing sobs. Sitting there alone in the bathroom, I began to realize why she was crying. My biggest fear was realized— my mother wasn't coming home. This must be what she was talking about before she went into the hospital. Aunt Dot came to me and said, "God needed a nurse in heaven so He took your mother." I was dumbfounded! I had no idea what this actually meant. But I did know that my mother was gone. I didn't really know exactly what her health problems were, but one of them, I learned much later, was a bleeding disorder, and she had bled to death on the operating table. In 1954 the medical world was not as knowledgeable as it is today, and the doctors couldn't save her.

I spent that night in a daze, riding on a train back to Ohio with my aunt crying beside me. I spent the trip hugging a doll that my mother had given me. When I arrived at our barrack-house in the middle of the night, my sisters were sleeping. My father was in the living room crying and my uncle Bob, who had a beer can in his hand, was there trying to console him. I discovered my sister Donna was sleeping in my bed, and as I crawled into her bed, I found wet sheets. I don't think I slept a wink that night.

In the morning, I could hear my father, my uncle, and my aunt Dot yelling at each other. I think my father and uncle were drinking. My aunt was blaming my father for my mother's death, yelling, "If you hadn't gotten her pregnant, she would still be alive." I heard a lot of noise and screaming and then the front door slammed. As I stood on tiptoes on the edge of my bed to look out the window, I saw Aunt Dot in her nightgown sitting on the lawn. My dad had thrown her, coffee cup and all, through the screen door, out into the front yard. He threw her luggage out after her. I remember the police being called, and they took her away in a cruiser instead of my father.

CHAPTER 3

the wheelers

We stayed in the barrack-home a little longer, I don't remember how long, perhaps a few weeks. Then my sisters and I were sent to live in the children's home run by the County of Ashtabula for a short time. Again, the smell of dried urine seemed to be everywhere. The place wasn't much different from the one in California. And, eventually, my sisters and I were split up, all being sent to live with different families. My dad went to live with his own abusive, alcoholic parents. I think my baby sister, Joyce, went with him for a while.

I went to stay with Thelma, my mother's best friend, her husband, Gordon Wheeler, and their daughter, Carol. Thelma was a stocky but pretty woman with dark Indian features. She was clearly the boss in the house. Her word was always the last. Gordon made me think of Superman, tall and handsome—he could do just about anything. He was always building and fixing things. Together, they were a committed family, and their daughter, Carol, who was five years my senior, was the love of their life. They loved children, and over the years, they took care of me and my sisters, as well as other children who needed help. I don't know why they never had more of their own kids.

Soon after I moved in there, I remember having a dream of being back in the barracks and sleeping in my bedroom with my sister. In the dream, my mother "flew" in the window (like an angel) to help me with my chores, like laundry and making beds. I hadn't forgotten her orders to me to "take care of Daddy and your sisters." I had several dreams like that the first year or so after her death. But, not being allowed to go to her funeral, I really didn't believe she was actually dead. I wasn't sure I knew what dead was, or where she actually was, but in my little six-year-old brain, I was convinced she would come back for us someday.

When I had those dreams about my mother, I usually wet the bed. Thelma and Gordon didn't have much compassion for bed-wetting, and once, they punished me by making me stay in bed, in my wet pajamas, all day. Still, it didn't teach me not to wet the bed. The smell of dried urine would trigger my memory of the orphanage in California, when my mother tried to commit suicide. When I asked Thelma about my mother, she would look away and try to change the subject. I could feel the tears welling up inside my eyes, but I got the message that I wasn't supposed to cry about it.

During the year I was in first grade, I developed some kind of eating problem. Today they would call it an eating disorder. For some reason, I just couldn't swallow my food, no matter how long I chewed it. I would sneak it under the table to the dog or wrap it in napkins and put it in the trash when no one was looking. But then I got caught giving part of a sandwich to the dog. The Wheelers seemed to have kind of rigid ideas about how children were supposed to behave. These ideas worked with their own daughter. So, they made a new sandwich and made me sit at the table for what seemed like hours, until I ate it all. I just couldn't get it down! Sometimes I was late for school because I couldn't swallow my toast, and they refused to write a note for the teacher because it was "my fault" for being late for school. So then I got in trouble at school, and got detention. When I got home, I got punished for getting detention. So, even if I did get my food down, I couldn't go out and play because I was being punished. And after being caught giving the dog my food, I was watched like a hawk while I ate. In fact, they didn't trust me at all. It seemed they questioned everything I did and didn't believe me most of the time.

One day, Gordon discovered one of Thelma's coveted rose plants had been trampled. I was their one and only suspect, and they wouldn't believe me when I said I didn't do it. Finally, they said that if I wouldn't admit my guilt, they were going to send me back to the children's home. They packed my suitcase and made me sit with it on the porch. When it was almost dark, and I was sitting there crying, scared to death, the next-door neighbor came over with his little boy, Danny. The neighbor said to Gordon, "My son here has something to say to you, Mr. Wheeler." Danny stammered "I . . . ah . . . er . . . I accidentally fell on your rosebush when I was playing today." Then, looking up at his father, who nodded toward Gordon, he said, "I'm sorry, Mr. and Mrs. Wheeler." They looked at me and said, "You're lucky this time!" They took my bags upstairs without one word of apology to me.

One thing that I can say was good about living there was their piano. I think I had music in my blood, and I could play anything I heard on the radio by ear. Even before I was big enough to get up on the bench on my own, I could play songs. So, they let me play their piano. I started taking lessons, but when the money ran out after about six weeks, I had to quit. I suspect my father refused to pay for the lessons. But music was, and always has been, a source of comfort and inner peace for me, especially when I create it.

Although living with the Wheelers was painful for me, I know now that they really didn't mean to hurt me. They did what they thought was best at the time. People weren't supposed to talk about their feelings back then. You were just supposed to suck it up and move on. So I learned to be strong. But somewhere inside my six-year-old soul, a rage was slowly building, like a tornado, quietly building strength enough to tear apart a whole town.

CHAPTER 4

moving around

During the next three years or so, my sisters and I were shuffled around to live with different families. I stayed with the Wheelers for about a year, and then moved on to someone else's house, where my mouth was cleaned out with soap when I wet the bed. On again to another place with the Starrett family. This time, my sister Donna was with me. Their daughter, Lezlie, who was my age, was happy to have a couple of girls to keep her company during the long winter months. They lived way out in the country in a town named Harpersfield, on a real farm with no plumbing in the house. They were warm, kind, wholesome people, and I recall that year as probably the best year of my childhood. I called them Mamma Ione and Daddy Nell. We fed the cows, pigs, and chickens, picked Concord grapes till dark in the fall, which they sold to Mogen David for wine, helped put animal feed up for the winter, and sat around and listened to the fireplace crackle at night. It was a simple, good life. Mamma was a lot like Thelma—loving and devoted, but quite stern. Daddy Nell was a good bit older then Mamma. He was very tall and slender, with a head full of unruly, curly locks of hair. He smoked cigarettes and had a nasty cough, but he was a kind, fun-loving soul. These people were honest and hardworking, albeit somewhat conservative and punitive at times. But if we were punished, we always knew what we were being punished for. And they never lied or broke promises to us. They didn't drink alcohol, and I didn't have to hide behind the couch in fear. They didn't put their fingers inside my panties. For the first time in my life, I felt like a normal kid.

Northeastern Ohio is in what's known as the "snow belt"; it can see as much as four feet of snow overnight in the winter. In the 1950s, snow clearance wasn't what it is today, and cars were all rear wheel drive, a fright to drive in snow and ice. The Thanksgiving we spent with Starretts brought a record snowfall. We were staying there for the holiday, and my father was going to drive out and eat Thanksgiving dinner with us. Daddy Nell didn't have a plow for his long driveway, so in order to keep the driveway clear for my dad's arrival, he rode up and down the driveway on his John Deere tractor. On one trip out to the road, he saw a car with Virginia plates in the ditch. He went over and discovered a newlywed couple on their honeymoon, who either had taken a seriously wrong turn or had no idea about the weather in the north. Neither of them was dressed properly for the weather, and the woman, probably suffering from hypothermia, was nearly unconscious. Daddy Nell put them both on his tractor and brought them up to the house. They spent Thanksgiving with us. Their honeymoon suite was the living room, complete with fold-out couch and fireplace. I remember getting admonished for peeking through the keyhole.

Even though life at the Starretts' was good, nonetheless, I started having a repetitive nightmare. In the dream, I am holding on to a string, at the end of which is an object about the size of a baseball. I start to swing it around and the object begins to get larger and larger. Eventually it becomes as large as a house and it is overtaking me. The dream was so frightening that I would cry out loud until someone would come and shake me awake. I would be all sweaty and confused and disoriented, and couldn't describe the dream in a way that made any sense. This dream plagued me well into my adult life. Many nights I would be afraid to go to sleep because I knew it would come again.

Another dream sequence would also follow me my whole life— dreams about being in water. One in particular would be of me alone in an ocean of cold, dark waves so high I couldn't see over them. I am always alone and just trying to tread water. I can't see land anywhere. I feel so overwhelmed and scared and alone. Other times I would dream of being in a house that is flooding, and I am floating and the water is rising and I am about to get pushed up to the ceiling. The water is always black.

I probably developed a sleep disorder as a result of forcing myself to stay awake at night, which most likely contributed to my difficulty in school.

Generally, no matter where we were living, my father would retrieve my sisters and me for holiday dinners with my relatives. I always dreaded these events. Literally all of the adults in my father's family were heavy drinkers. The men became mean and sometimes violent when they drank too much. Oftentimes there were frightening arguments between my uncles and my father, sometimes ending in physical confrontations and hasty, tire-squealing exits from the house, with children crying in the backseat.

Usually, while sitting around in the living room before or after dinner, I had to sit on my grandfather's lap while he stuck his hands into my panties and sort of "tickled" me—just like my uncle Bob had done in the car trip from California. I hated it—I hated the feeling it gave me, but I was also confused by it. I mean, physically it sometimes actually felt good! But, at the same time, it made me feel icky. And because he would whisper to me not to tell anyone, I eventually figured out that it wasn't right. I really had no idea what was going on. I didn't notice whether it was happening to anyone else, and I was embarrassed and afraid that someone might see. I sometimes thought I saw my uncle Bob giving my grandfather a "knowing" look. But he looked at me like that, too! I always wondered, Why do they do this, and why am I not supposed to tell? I was afraid that if someone else saw, they might blame me. But I didn't know how to stop it. He would always tell me I was special and that I couldn't tell anyone. How could the women in the family not have seen what was going on? Nobody, not even my father, seemed to care what was happening to me. Maybe, once they had enough to drink, they saw things the way they wanted to see them, instead of the way they really were.

CHAPTER 5

h o u s e k e e p e r s

The summer before I went into fourth grade, we moved back with my father in our little house on Myrtle Avenue in Ashtabula. It was a house my parents were having built just before my mother died, but after her death, my father rented it out to tenants for a few years. (We called the street "Fertile Myrtle," because in the twenty-eight houses on the street there were about seventy-five kids!) After we moved in, I met some of the kids in the neighborhood, and became friends with the Mello kids next door, with Lynn next door to them, and with Becky next door to Lynn. We were all pretty much the same age, and Lynn was in my class in school. These friendships would come to be very special to me as the years progressed.

My father realized we were too young to take care of ourselves when he was at work, so he decided a housekeeper would be what he needed. However, I don't think he knew how to hire one, or he just didn't pay enough to get a good one.

The first woman I remember coming to take care of us was an old woman who dressed like she was out of the 1800s. She had never seen an electric stove or washing machine before, and she tried to light a wood fire in the oven! She lasted about two days. I'm not sure if she quit or was fired. The next woman was named Mary Brady. She had three sons who had been removed from her by the State for abuse; they were sent to live in Boys Town in Nebraska. In some ways she was nice, but she liked to hit us with a switch that she made us go out and cut from the tree when we were "bad." I think she liked to drink my dad's beer also, which made him angry. During the summer, I traveled on a train with her to Boys Town to see her sons. (This was great —it meant getting away from my father.) She lasted about a year.

Then came Eva. She was a little older and she liked to drink alcohol. She drank all of my dad's beer and refilled the bottles with water. When he discovered it, he was furious. She lived with us, and my dad would give her the weekends off to do whatever she wanted. One weekend, she didn't come back until Tuesday, when she stumbled, drunk, into the neighbor's kitchen (thinking she was in our house). She fell onto their floor in front of a shocked family eating their dinner. She was immediately fired. The woman whose kitchen Eva fell into took pity on us and sent her sister, Sylvia, over to meet us. My dad hired her right away. She had four kids and was recently divorced. She didn't live with us, but she came every day with her kids. She cleaned, cooked, and did the laundry. I really liked her—I wanted a mother so much.

Sylvia and my father started having sex. I saw them one night on my way to the bathroom (although, at the time, I didn't know what they were doing). Her ex-husband was a wild man who had been in and out of prison. And he wanted her back. When he got wind of the fact that she was spending days and evenings at our house, he blew his cork! One Saturday afternoon, I got out of the shower, wrapped myself in a towel, and walked through the hallway to my bedroom. There I discovered Sylvia, her kids, and my sisters sitting on the floor, with the telephone stretched around into the hallway. They put their fingers to their lips and shushed me when I asked what was going on.

Sylvia's husband was at the back door. He was drunk, and he had a gun. He had cut the wires to the telephone, so my dad had jumped out of a window to go to the neighbor's house to call the police. I remember Sylvia's husband banging on the door, yelling, "Woman, you get your damn ass out here now, or I'm coming in to get you!" The cops came and hauled him away. But I was scared to death every time Sylvia came to our house after that.

One sunny afternoon, the police came and arrested my father. As it turns out, Sylvia was pregnant, and she had charged my father with something called "breach of promise" for promising to marry her and then backing out. He apparently was never formally charged with a crime and was sent home. But we never saw Sylvia again.

For years after this, my father got cards in the mail from "Your son, Danny," Sylvia's son, a child my dad denied fathering. I never met him.

CHAPTER 6

my father

I think I was in fifth or sixth grade when I began having "real-life nightmares." My father decided I could do him a favor. He convinced me that I looked just like my mother, and because I reminded him of her, I could serve him the same way she did. He came into my bedroom one night, crawled into my bed, and made me hold his erect penis. Then he spread my legs and forced it into me. This became a regular event whenever he felt like it. Really, I should say he was raping me. It certainly was not consensual. In addition to intercourse, he sometimes did really awful things, like masturbating me with a kielbasa sausage, or making me give him oral sex. I never knew when he would come into my room and demand sex. He always called it "our relations," and he told me never to tell anyone. He was usually drunk when he came into my room, and I learned to hate the smell of whisky. I began to think that maybe this was what my mother meant when she told me the day before she died to "take care of your daddy and sisters, because you are the oldest." I can't remember if it hurt or exactly what I felt during these sessions. I guess I blocked the pain of these events, because they were just too traumatic. I don't think he did it to my sisters. Just me.

About the same time, my uncle Bob began coming to our house when I was alone. He made me do the same thing that I had to do with my father. He reminded me of our "special secret" from before. I didn't understand anything about sex, except for seeing my dad and Sylvia that night (and I really didn't see what they were doing). I didn't know it had anything to do with having babies. I didn't know how people got pregnant. Now I was carrying so many secrets, I had a hard time keeping them all straight. I couldn't tell my father about my uncle Bob because they were both doing the same thing to me. I couldn't tell my friends Lynn and Becky because I was told never to tell anyone. Also, I didn't think they would like me anymore if I told them.

On the nights that these things would happen, I began to have dreams about flying. Not in an airplane, but just flying, like Peter Pan. I'd fly out my bedroom window and down the street, looking down at the roofs of the houses. I even saw the roof of my school, and I could see the beach on Lake Erie from the air. I loved these dreams; they made me feel free and somehow safe. But the other nightmares also continued, and I would long for the flying dreams.

Toward the end of fifth grade, I started my menstrual period. I had no idea what was going on until my girlfriend Lynn told her mother. Her mother talked to me about menstruation and gave me a little book to read. But I still didn't know it had any connection to having babies. I had no women in my life to tell me these things. My aunt Dot in Pittsburgh was not available to me due to the geographical distance, not to mention her mental disorder. (Everyone in the family said she was "crazy.") My uncles (my father's two brothers) were also both alcoholics. And, as I have already mentioned, they were not safe to be around, either. Their wives were too busy with their own families to try to be a mother to us. I was trapped.

The next person my dad hired to take care of us was a woman named Cecile. She was married, had two teenage sons, and lived just a block away. She would come over to clean house, and she was there when we came home from school. She would start dinner for us, then she would go home. It seemed as though things might get somewhat "normal" at my house with Cecile there. But the downside was that she occasionally brought her husband, Pete, with her. There was something about him that gave me the creeps. I must have had the word *victim* written on my forehead because he, too, began sexually abusing me. His little fetish was to lift me up and lay me on top of the upright piano that was in the basement (which was about five feet high) and do things to me with his mouth. It made me sick to my stomach. But I was scared to death that if I didn't cooperate with him, he would just push me off the piano onto the cement floor. He smelled of chewing tobacco, alcohol, and sweat. I hated him, and Cecile, too, because she brought him with her. So now, I had to watch out for my father, my uncles, my grandfather, and Pete.

My father's drinking escalated during this time, and he was like Dr. Jekyll/Mr. Hyde when he drank. He was a mean drunk. He would take his belt off and swing it around, whipping us with it, sometimes with the buckle end. We all learned to pay attention to whether or not he was drunk when he came home every day, and we tried to just be quiet and stay out of his way if he was drinking. But it wasn't always possible. He was totally unpredictable, as well as unreliable when it came to keeping promises. Being the oldest, and still believing that I had to follow my mother's dying wishes, I usually did a lot of the chores, housekeeping, and cooking. But I could never do it to my father's satisfaction. Nothing ever seemed good enough for him. We had to sit and wait for him to come to inspect the kitchen after doing the dishes, and if the floor wasn't swept to perfection, we would have to do it over.

Mealtimes were also quite interesting in our house. My father was obsessed with eating sounds. We were strictly forbidden to chew with our mouths open, or talk with our mouths full. Either of these infractions would surely bring a fist in the mouth from him. He also would listen to see how loud we chewed our food, and he would tell us to chew it more quietly. It got so that we were afraid to eat crunchy vegetables like celery or carrots. We didn't talk at the dinner table, either, because no matter what we said, it would somehow start an argument. My father became famous for picking up his plate of food and throwing it across the table at one of us. We got very good at ducking so the plate would hit the wall, with spaghetti running down the wall afterward. Sometimes we would laugh at this behavior—I'm sure this was one of our coping mechanisms to deal with our fear. But, of course, our laughter would only stir up more rage in him. The laughter could quickly be turned into tears with one blow from my father's hand, or one sentence, like "Okay, you're not going out to the football game tonight!" My father spoiled more of my teenage activities than I can even remember. So, we learned to stifle our laughter.

We were always afraid to bring friends home because we never knew how my father would react or treat them. My best friends, Lynn and Becky, seemed to take my father's behavior in stride. Becky's mother was divorced and worked two jobs to make ends meet for five kids. Becky was the oldest in her family, too, and she and I had a lot in common. I wish I could have gotten to know her mother better, but she was always out working. Lynn's father drank, but she had a mother and what I considered a normal household. We were all best friends throughout high school, which is one of the things that made life bearable. Although I never told them about the things that went on in my house, my friendship with them was one of the reasons I survived this time in my life.

Following my mother's death, her mother, my grandmother Fulwider, tried to spend as much time with us as she could. However, Perry, the man she lived with, was a mean, violent alcoholic. For some reason, he didn't like us and he forbade her to see us or come to our house. But she loved us—and we loved her. She came to see us anyway, and she always suffered for it. I remember once she arrived at our house with a broken nose, and she told my father that Perry had done it. Another time, she had her arm in a sling. Other times, she walked several blocks, hiding her car on another street so Perry wouldn't see it near our house. But, finally, he went too far.

She died in a Cleveland hospital after a severe beating from Perry. The police found chunks of her scalp and hair on dresser drawer knobs. For reasons I never learned, Perry was never charged with any crime.

I remember the day that my dad allowed him to come to our house and sit with the three of us in the living room to tell us a "story" of how my grandmother died. He sat in a chair in the living room, and my sisters and I sat on the floor to listen to him. "She was sick and fell out of bed and hit her head. I picked her up and put her back into bed, and she fell out again. When I couldn't wake her up, I called an ambulance. But she was in a coma and never came out of it." I never believed his story. I was actually scared of him, so I stayed quiet. I hated him.

Losing Grandma Fulwider was a huge blow to us. She was all we had left after losing our mother. We loved her so much. Now it seemed we were becoming more and more alone in the world. A few years later, Perry was found beaten to death behind a bar. No one was ever charged with his death.

My father suffered frequent mental breakdowns, probably due to his experiences in the prison camps during World War II, as well as abuse from his own parents. Often, he would have to go to the psychiatric ward at the veterans' hospital for days, weeks, or sometimes even months. During these times, the Wheelers would rescue us and take us to their house. I always felt they cared for us, and it always seemed amazing to me that they would appear just when we needed them. To the best of my knowledge, they never asked my dad for money or any other form of payment for taking care of us. If they hadn't stepped in during those times, the State would have taken us away. I've always wondered if that would have been better.

During my father's psychiatric hospitalizations, he was frequently allowed to have weekend passes from the hospital. The doctor said he shouldn't have all three of his kids with him because it would be too stressful, but one child, preferably the oldest, would be good company for him over these weekends. The first time Thelma told me I was to go home alone for the weekend with my father, I cringed. I really didn't want to go.

Her response was, "Shame on you for not wanting to go take care of your daddy!"

So I went. Those weekends were horrible. Thelma and Gordon didn't know what they were sending me home to. In fact, most people thought my father was just a wonderful guy; they would say things like, "taking care of his kids after losing his wife like that."

By the time I entered my adolescent years, it seemed that each morning I woke up thinking I couldn't endure another day. I began having thoughts of suicide on a daily basis. But then I would remember my mother's instructions, and so I kept putting one foot in front of the other to make it through another day.

One day, I came home from school and found my father sitting in the kitchen with our next-door neighbor, Mr. Northrop, who was a little younger than my father and quite good-looking. He and his wife had two kids, for whom I babysat frequently. They were nice people.

While I stood at the kitchen sink washing vegetables for supper, my father told me to sit down, that he wanted to talk to me. I looked at him and then Mr. Northrop, confused and scared. My father said, "I think you are pregnant and Mr. Northrop here is the father!" I had no idea what he was talking about. I was still somewhat unclear about how babies were made at this point, but I knew I was *not* pregnant. There was no reason for this suspicion, except maybe my father was watching when I had my periods. Perhaps he thought they were not regular enough and he was afraid *he* had gotten me pregnant, and so he wanted to blame someone else. Mr. Northrop had never touched me, nor was he the type of person to do so. He was horrified at my father's accusations, and I'm surprised he didn't file a lawsuit. He and his wife put their house up for sale and moved away shortly after that.

I was completely mortified. I never knew what my father was going to come up with next. It didn't seem safe for me to walk on the earth. At this point, suicide began taking over my entire thought process. It seemed like the only way out. I began thinking of ways to do it.

My father had favorite names for all of us. One of his favorites was "Ignoramus." Whenever any of us made a mistake, or didn't quite muster up to his expectations, he would yell, "You stupid Ignoramus!" Another one was "you stupid individual!" I don't ever remember him telling us we were good, smart, or pretty—ever! I can recall one morning when I was about thirteen, coming out to the breakfast table in tears because my hair was totally unmanageable. I had gotten a perm, and it was nothing but frizz. My father made some comment he thought to be funny and my sisters laughed. With tears stinging my eyes, I blurted out, "It's not funny!" My father called me a slut and hauled off and backhanded me across the face so hard I thought I felt my brain move! A couple of days after that, he had one of his mental meltdowns and went to the veterans' psychiatric unit and we went to stay with the Wheelers again.

At the Wheelers' house, I noticed that the place where my father had slapped my face had begun to swell up. I didn't think much of it because I was getting used to being slapped around, and I often had painful bruises and welts that I tried to hide or cover up.

While we were staying at the Wheelers' house, Thelma's mother was dying of breast cancer. It was a terrible time for them, and I can't imagine why they took us in. But they did. We went with them to Thelma's mother's house almost every day, and needless to say, we weren't their top priority. We were just sent outside to play on our own. No one seemed to notice my swelling face. It felt like a giant toothache, and it got so bad that I was having trouble opening my mouth. So I put myself on a city bus and went downtown to the dentist's office. They weren't very anxious to treat me because, as they were quick to point out, my father hadn't paid our bill. But because the swelling had spread down below my jaw, into my neck, I was having difficulty breathing, and I couldn't get my mouth open to talk, they helped me. After X-rays were taken, they determined that I had a blood clot the size of a quarter lodged between a tooth and a bone—and it was getting larger. They thought it might have come from a blow to the face. No one questioned me, at least I can't remember them questioning me, about possible child abuse. I don't think they did anything about child abuse back then. If your father hit you, it was okay. After several phone calls to get the appropriate authorization from my father in the psychiatric hospital, they anesthetized me and removed *all* of my bottom teeth on the right side. There was never any plan to get me a partial plate or bridge to prevent the upper teeth from falling out of their sockets. So, for the better part of my adult life, I had no teeth on the bottom right side of my mouth. The upper teeth dropped down, touching the gums. I gradually stopped smiling because you could see the empty space in the side of my mouth, and I was extremely embarrassed by it, a constant reminder of my childhood experiences.

CHAPTER 7

family affairs

Ashtabula, Ohio, was right on Lake Erie, with its beautiful beaches. It was customary for teenagers to spend summer days at the beach. In the sixties, little cotton two-piece bathing suits were all the rage, not those string bikinis they wear now. The only thing that showed was a little abdominal skin above the belly button. I had learned to sew and made most of my clothes, and I had made a cute little gingham bathing suit, which I was very proud of. I tried so hard to fit into the rest of the world, and to just be normal. Upon arriving home from the beach one day, all sunburned and greasy from suntan lotion, I walked into the kitchen to find my father sitting with a man who looked like a homeless bum. They were drinking, and were quite intoxicated. As I passed by the table, the bum reached out, grabbed me, and pulled me onto his lap, putting his slimy hand into the top of my bathing suit. I pushed at him, trying to break free, and my father bellowed at me, "How dare you treat one of my friends that way? You're a disrespectful, ungrateful little brat!" I was banished to my bedroom (thankfully). These incidents only contributed to my confusion, depression, and suicidal thoughts. I felt like I was trapped in hell and death seemed like the only way out.

My sister Donna watched me as I began my adolescent years, wanting to go out with friends, go on dates, or even go to church. She decided that she didn't want to do any of those things because of how difficult my father made it for me. As a result, except for one date at the senior prom, Donna didn't date at all during high school. She became involved at the YWCA, got on the swim team, became a lifeguard, and learned scuba diving. What a wonderful way to escape! But Donna was quiet and kept to herself. I don't know what her perception of our family experience was—maybe it was not the same as mine. But I suspect she was having trouble sleeping, too.

Life with our father was like walking on eggshells in a minefield. I was afraid to go to sleep; I was afraid to wake up. I was afraid to do anything for fear of his reaction. When he was drinking, anything was possible. When he wasn't drinking, anything was possible.

One Thanksgiving, he went into a rage about something, and he sent all three of us to the basement and locked the door. Initially, we were smirking and trying to stifle giggles, making fun of him for being such a loony. But inside we were a little sad and scared. He was crying and stomping around the house saying he had his gun and would kill himself because he couldn't stand us anymore. (I was secretly hoping he would do it.) The raw turkey, planned for Thanksgiving, sat all day in the kitchen sink. The three of us, sitting in the basement all day, had to be extremely quiet so as not to trigger an outrage in him. At some point during the day, we saw Thelma and Gordon Wheeler's feet walk by the basement windows and heard them ring the doorbell. Apparently they had stopped in for a visit. But we were afraid to make any noise, so we sat in silence, looking out the basement window, desperately hoping they would notice us, come in the house, and rescue us. But they left, thinking we had gone away for the day. My father never did shoot himself or anybody else with his gun, but living with the fear that he would do it was worse than hearing it go off.

Another time, he went into a rage and said he couldn't stand to be our father anymore. He packed a suitcase, took his gun, and said he was leaving us. I don't know where he planned to go, but he went out to the car and took off. When it was time to go to bed, we turned out the lights and locked the door with the chain, like we always did, then went to bed. I was glad he was gone! Then, at about 3:00 a.m., we heard a crash as my drunken father kicked the door in, cutting his foot on the broken glass in the process, leaving a trail of blood through the house. I lay in bed in stark terror, afraid that he would come in and shoot me because he was so angry that we had locked him out. But he just went into his bedroom and cried. If I hadn't hated him so much, sometimes I might have felt sorry for him. He had suffered a lot in his life, having grown up in an abusive, alcoholic family, as well as having experienced extreme conditions in a prison camp during World War II. My sister Donna, the quiet member of the family, always felt sorry for him and would try to console him during these episodes. (To this day, she is still his biggest advocate.) But my hatred for him only grew.

He would sometimes have terrible nightmares about his experiences in the war, and talk in his sleep. I would hear him yelling things like, "Over there—look, there's a light. Get behind that pile of wood, quick! They've spotted us—we have to run!" Once, when I went into his room to wake him out of his dream, he pulled me into bed with him. I didn't try to help him again.

He never really got over my mother's death. He would cry every time he talked about her. Christmas was always hard. We had an angel for the top of our Christmas tree that was made out of spun glass. It was nothing really spectacular, but we thought she was beautiful. Somewhere along the line, we began to think she was our mother sitting up there on the tree, watching out for us. It was a distorted little fantasy.

I really came to hate Christmas. We always got together with my father's family. The dinner would always start out great. There were good cooks in the family, and the food was delicious. But then the alcohol would begin to flow, and personalities would start to change. Often, the evening would end up in a drunken fight with people yelling at each other and leaving in a huff with kids and babies crying. And, as usual, during the day or evening, one or all of the men would find a way to get me alone so they could stick their dirty fingers in my panties! It didn't matter where we had dinner, it usually wasn't safe for me.

My one saving grace with these family affairs was my cousin David. He was my age, and my uncle Bob was his stepfather. He wasn't really a blood cousin, but I always thought of him as my cousin. He was a good friend, as well. Sometimes he went with his grandparents on holidays. But when he was at our get-togethers, I was safe because I stuck to him like glue, and the men didn't bother me. During our teenage years, we spent a lot of time together. I remember once when we were twelve or thirteen, we were up in the attic, snooping around. I found some pictures that had been taken at my mother's funeral. There she was, lying in a casket, dead. I think this was when I knew for sure she was dead. It was such a blow. My cousin David had lost his father in early childhood, and he seemed to understand. But David's life at home wasn't much better than mine. I suspect that he was being abused by his stepfather, the same uncle who was abusing me. My uncle had developed a friendship with a strange man named John Silo who lived out in the country. Sometimes we all went out there for Sunday dinners. John Silo was a very weird guy, and I remember my father saying once that he thought John was a "queer." I didn't actually know what that meant, but I didn't ask. He was creepy, though, and my uncle spent a lot of time with him. I've always suspected that my cousin David was abused by the two of them. When he graduated from high school, David left Ashtabula and never, ever went back. I never saw him again.

CHAPTER 8

n o t - s o - s w e e t   s i x t e e n

By ninth grade, my little group of friends expanded to four, with a girl who lived a few blocks away named Mary. One Sunday, Lynn and Mary invited me to go to church with them. My previous church experiences had consisted of being dropped off at a Baptist church by my father once in a while. He would put our hair up in "spoolies" the night before, get us dressed up, and just drop us off. He never went himself. This was his idea of giving us religion. I always hated it and really had no interest in church. But when my two best friends said that it was a lot of fun, I went with them. They went to Messiah Lutheran Church and belonged to the Luther League—an organization for teenagers. I loved the music, the people, and the place. For some reason, I felt safe there. There were kids my age who didn't go to my school, didn't know my father, or where I lived. There were adults who didn't look at me in that funny way that people in my neighborhood did. They treated me with respect and didn't judge me.

I went to a Luther League beach party one night, and had more fun than I had ever had in my life! The minister, Pastor Petterson, was my father's age, a big, jolly man who was very kind to me. He showed up at the Luther League affairs and just blended in with the kids. Once, we had a picnic out in the country at a parishioner's house. As a joke, a bunch of us rolled Pastor Petterson's Volkswagen Bug into the cornfield and then stood the cornstalks up so he couldn't see where it went. He took it all in stride and played along with the game. I had never known an adult who could be so kind and understanding, or who wanted kids to have fun. He even allowed us to learn about other religions. As my high school years progressed, I came to care a great deal for him, and probably could have confided in him about my home life. But I was really afraid that I was the guilty one and it would be considered my fault—and I believed that

I would end up in jail or a reformatory. So I never told anyone.

Keeping my secrets inside created a lot of pain for me, and I began to have trouble coping with day-to-day life. I started skipping school once in a while. Instead, I would go to the church and sit up in the balcony for hours alone, usually crying. Sometimes I went down to the church basement and played the piano. It became my safe haven. My father began to question my allegiance to the church, and I imagine he thought I had confided in the minister about "our relations." So I always had to fight with him to get to go to services or activities. He used this for punishment whenever we disagreed or argued about anything, and I missed many important events because my father decided not to let me go. (Sometimes I jumped out my bedroom window, and went anyway!) My sisters went to church with me occasionally, but I don't think it was as important to them as it was to me.

It was at Messiah Lutheran Church where I met the love of my life, Dick Forringer. He was a freshman at Kent State University. There was something about him that went straight into my heart and soul. I instinctively knew I could trust him, and I fell in love with him—at least what I thought was love. I had been on a few dates with other boys, but nothing that amounted to anything. For some reason, Dick was all I could think about. He was attracted to me as well, but not with the same intensity. He was engaged to a girl named Shirley, and she went to Luther League activities with us. But then one day I found out that Dick had broken off his engagement with Shirley.

We went bowling on our first date. I didn't know it until I got there, but I was to be the substitute team member for Shirley, who had quit the league because of her breakup with Dick. Dick and I started dating and courted for a couple of years while I was in high school. I wasn't interested in any boys from my school—just Dick. He was all I thought about.

After I got to know his mother, Freda, I discovered that we had been neighbors back in 1953 when we returned from California, just before my mother's death. I thought Dick's mother was an angel sent to me. She was the first person to actually talk to me about my mother. I could vaguely remember playing with Dick and other kids back then. But I took this as a sign that we were meant to be together. Dick believed people should maintain their virginity before marriage, so he never tried to "go all the way with me", although we did get into some heavy petting. I really didn't understand it, but he made me feel safe. All I really wanted was for him to love me and take me away from my father. I don't think he understood (nor did I) the complicated feelings I had. I never told him about the incest, because then he would know I wasn't a virgin and wouldn't marry me. As I look back, I realize my expectations of him were unrealistic. But, at the time, he was my Prince Charming, and my relationship with him helped me to feel a little closer to normal.

Sometime during the tenth grade, I learned something that would change me forever. During a vocabulary lesson in English class one day, I learned the definition of *incest*. Until then, I had no idea that what was going on in my house was considered taboo or was illegal. I thought that maybe other girls had to do this with their father too. When I saw this in print, my heart began racing and I couldn't concentrate. I left the school in a daze, walking for what seemed like miles along the shores of Lake Erie. (Our high school was right on the shore.) I didn't want to ever go home again. I wanted to die. I had no one to talk to and nowhere to go. I had these terrible secrets that I now could never tell, because they were illegal! It would be like confessing that I had robbed a bank, or killed someone! I truly believed I would be sent to jail, me instead of my father and uncles and grandfather. I didn't know what to do. Suicide seemed the best option. On this day, I made the decision that I would never let any of them touch me again!

There were those times when my father tried, in his own way, to be a good dad to us, when he was sober, that is. One of them was on November 22, 1963—the day that President Kennedy was assassinated. I had stayed home from school that day with a sore throat, and I was lying on the couch, watching daytime sitcoms on TV. The show was interrupted with an announcement that President Kennedy had been killed in Dallas, Texas. I was alone and I remember feeling scared. I just cried and cried. I had actually seen him during a campaign trip to Ashtabula. He stood on the steps of the City Hall and gave a wonderful speech, and I was in the audience. After his death, they engraved his famous quote, "Ask not what your country can do for you, but what you can do for your country," on the front of the steps. Everyone had such high hopes for our country's future with President Kennedy.

When the rest of the family came home that day, my sister Donna took it the hardest. She couldn't be consoled. She was only thirteen, but somehow the idea of our leader being killed really shook her to the bone. Seeing Donna's pain, my father decided to reach out and ask for help in dealing with our grief. Joe Torma was our Sealtest milkman, and he and his family of twelve children had become friends of ours. They were the nicest people in the world; even as poor as they were, they would give you the shirts off their backs. So, uninvited, we went over to their house. When we got there, they welcomed us with open arms, prayed with us and shared some of their Catholic-based spiritual wisdom with us, in an attempt to soften our pain. I didn't really understand what they were talking about most of the time, but it was their kindness and caring that mattered the most. That, and the fact that my father actually cared about us! As I look back, I realized that my father had no clue how to console someone or to tap into any kind of spirituality. He was in his own dark world most of the time.

The other thing that our father tried to do to make us a family and to have fun was to take us camping in the summer. Once we went to the Smokey Mountains and we had a blast! But we usually went to a state park that was on the border of Ohio and Pennsylvania, on Pymatuming Lake. There was one summer I'll never forget. My dad let each of us bring along a friend—that meant six girls together with my dad in charge. His planning skills weren't the greatest, and he had been drinking the whole day we were to leave. We didn't actually get on the road until evening, and our destination was several hours' drive away. Arriving well after closing time, we were let in by a security guard and told to pitch our camp anywhere. We were to go to see the park ranger in the morning for a permanent site and to settle up the money. So, in the dark, trying to be quiet so as not to wake other campers, we put the tent up and went to sleep. In the morning, I awoke to a terrible stench and a lot of noise. As I looked around, I noticed that my father wasn't in the tent. I looked outside and saw that we were sleeping in between the bathrooms and the playground! We weren't even in a real campsite. I noticed that my father was nowhere to be found. He had going fishing. (Obviously, we were not his priority). So, being accustomed to taking charge in his absence, I went and talked to the park ranger about our predicament. With raised eyebrows, he assigned us a better campsite and said we could pay up later. All six of us packed up the tent and gear, I drove the car (which I had never done before) to the new site, and we were all set up before lunchtime. Noon came and went, and my father didn't return. I figured he was drunk somewhere, and didn't really give it much thought. We ate lunch, went swimming, and met other kids in the campground.

Then, about 5:00 or so, as I was trying to figure out what to make for supper, a car pulled up, and out stepped my father with a single boat oar in his hand. He was in his bare feet and sunburned like a cooked lobster. He was drunk. He had taken his booze with him in the boat, and in a drunken stupor, had fallen asleep. His boat had drifted over to the other side of the lake. He was awakened by the boat bumping up against some rocks. When he "came to" he discovered he had lost an oar and he couldn't get the motor started. He eventually found some people who gave him a ride around the lake and back to the campground. Needless to say, there weren't any fish in his bucket. But, despite this, and many other situations my father got us into, I still like camping to this day. And even though those trips were mostly fun, it was impossible for me to ever trust my father or to believe he was sincere. It was always like waiting for the other shoe to drop.

I can't remember when, but another man eventually came creeping into my life. At first, I considered him a friend and a safe person. He was the mailman. On summer days he always stopped and talked to me; he seemed like such a nice guy. I learned that he was married and lived a few blocks away, and that he had a daughter with polio who lived in an iron lung. I knew about iron lungs because my mother had worked in a polio hospital in California, and she used to take me to work with her once in a while. People with polio sometimes lose the muscle strength to breathe, so they devised these chambers that looked like water heaters laying on their side to assist the patients to breathe. It seemed like a horrible life for the people who had to live in them, but I guess the doctors kept hoping for a cure for polio. Anyway, somehow this made me think the mailman was a nice person, not like all the other men I knew.

While walking in a blizzard on my way home from school one day, I saw his car pull up and he offered me a ride home. I gladly accepted. Wrong thing to do. He didn't drive to our street, but instead, to a secluded area in a park. He stopped the car, muckled on to me, and began kissing me. I was horrified and outraged, but mostly disappointed that he was just like all the men in my family. I pushed him away and said very clearly, "You can't do this with me! Leave me alone—take me home!" To my surprise, he started the car and took me home.

I got out of the car without saying a word, hoping I would never have to see him again. A couple of days later, while walking home from school with a girlfriend, Diane, I saw him in his car, slowing down and looking over at me as we walked. I remember my heart beating faster—I was so scared. Why would he follow me? I ran into a store where there were other people to hide from him. Diane asked me what was wrong—she said I looked like I had seen a ghost. I ended up telling her what he had done (but not the rest of my secrets). She went home and told her mother, who in turn called my father. The next day, when my father came home from work, he told me that Diane's mother had called him and told him that I had been having sex with the mailman! I couldn't get him to believe the truth, and he began accusing me of soliciting sex, and calling me a slut. I started crying and couldn't stop. Part of me was so confused—he was the one having sex with me! And I didn't solicit it! I couldn't figure this out. But I had vowed no one would ever touch me again—sexually or otherwise. I ran from him when he tried to hit me for "talking back."

During the year I was sixteen, I made an attempt at suicide by taking a whole bottle of aspirin. Today I know that a whole bottle of aspirin can be lethal, or at the very least, can severely damage your liver. But I only got dizzy from it. Nothing else happened. I was disappointed, and wondered just how I could kill myself. I didn't have the courage to cut my wrists, and I had no clue how to do anything else. But suicide was all I thought about for the next several years. I just couldn't see how I would live the rest of my life with all this pain and fear, and the tormenting nightmares that continued night after night. Many nights, I would go to sleep crying or in some weird way trying to talk to my mother. I missed her so much. I felt like I was slowly going nuts.

Learning to drive became a goal for me. But it wasn't easy. My father was a yelling, controlling tyrant who expected me to know how to drive the car the minute I sat in the driver's seat. I remember my first driving experience with him. It was a warm Sunday afternoon. As we were all on our way to my grandmother's house, my father asked me, "How would you like to drive the car out to Grandma's house today?" My sisters, sitting in the backseat, looked terrified, as was I. But I wanted to learn to drive. So I said, "Sure." I had gotten my learner's permit, but I had not yet driven (except for that time at the campground). He stopped the car on the side of the road. I slid into the driver's seat and waited for him to tell me what to do. He yelled, "So what are you waiting for? Drive the car!" I turned the key and held it too long, causing the car to make that awful ratcheting sound it does when you don't let go soon enough. This produced a bark from my father to let go of the key. I struggled with the shifter on the column, but eventually got the car into Drive. I pushed on the gas and made the tires spin, sending gravel out from under the car. Again, my father yelled at me not to push on the gas so hard, and I slammed on the brake, almost putting everyone through the windshield. No seatbelts in those days.

That was the way it went most of the trip, until I got used to the pressure needed on the gas pedal and the brake. When we got to my grandmother's house, I didn't make a sharp enough turn into her driveway, and I slammed on the brakes to avoid hitting a tree. By this time my sisters were crying, and I was shaking like a leaf. My father was yelling at the top of his lungs, and I began crying. I turned the car off and got out, took my learner's permit out of my wallet, and tore it into tiny pieces. I didn't want any more driving lessons with him. I could wait until I was older and had someone else to teach me. When we got into my grandmother's house, he launched into a litany of what a "stupid Ignoramus" I was (his favorite name for us). My grandmother and grandfather just laughed!

When it was time to go home, I climbed into the backseat. My father demanded that I get back into the driver's seat and drive home. "I don't have a learner's permit anymore—I can't!"

"I don't give a damn about your learner's permit—you're driving this car home!" he said. And I did, with my terrified sisters in the backseat.

Later that year, I tried again to learn to drive with my friend Mary helping me. She had a lot of patience teaching me how to use a clutch. Her mother took me to take the road test, but I flunked it. It would be many years before I sat behind the wheel of a car again.

CHAPTER 9

girlfriends

Incidents like the driving lesson from my father fed the huge, ugly, dark rage that was building inside of me. I didn't realize this wasn't normal. There were many times when I lost my temper and went right into a full-blown panic attack. When this would happen, I would mentally melt down, saying and doing things I later regretted. The rage began to define my character, and people began saying I was living proof that redheads had fiery tempers. My anger was also how I kept myself away from my perpetrators but it chased everyone away from me, including people I wanted to be friends with. Only my best friends, Becky, Lynn, and Mary stuck by me. They are probably the reason I made it through high school. But they must have thought I was crazy. *I* thought I was crazy. I *was* crazy!

My father spent a lot of money on racy cars and alcohol, and my wish to take piano lessons was not his priority, even though he was a musician himself. So I began taking informal lessons from Sandy, a girl I knew from school who played for the choir. She began spending a little time with me after school, teaching me to read notes, and she also gave me some sheet music. I began playing on our old upright piano in the basement (the one Pete Kirkey made me lie on top of). I learned to play some of the popular songs of the sixties. Playing these pieces made me feel free and alive in that moment. I also began to write some songs of my own, most of which were sad pieces that sounded like funeral dirges. The music seemed to represent my painful journey in life. I would close my eyes and see myself walking alone in the dark, then play music that reflected how lonely I felt and how hopeless my life seemed. In some way, this was my therapy. I have to say, music was, and continues to be, one of my greatest joys in life.

I also sang in the choirs at school and church. At Christmastime every year, there was a citywide choir that rehearsed for a few weeks and then performed Handel's *Messiah* on Christmas Eve. I felt honored to be able to sing with those people, but my father never came to any of my performances.

My father had begun dating, and he had several "girlfriends," which was a huge relief to me because it meant he was no longer bothering me for sex. Some of the women in his life were good to my sisters and me. But something always eventually happened to ruin the relationship.

Virginia came along when I was about sixteen or seventeen, and we all really liked her. She had teenage kids also, and sometimes we all went on picnics together. Virginia worked at the Singer sewing store, so I had the opportunity to pick up more sewing skills from her. She seemed empathetic to the fact that we were three girls without a mother. I don't know if she ever figured out "the truth" about my father, but she was awfully good to us. Then, just as every other nice person in our life had done, one day she disappeared. I later learned that she had gotten pregnant. In the 1960s, it wasn't socially acceptable to have a baby without a husband, especially if you were divorced and had kids already. I was told that she went to a home for unwed mothers somewhere far away and she ultimately gave the baby up for adoption. So there was another sibling I would never meet. We also never saw Virginia again, at least not at our house. I did see her on my own when I got older and went to work in a store uptown near where she worked. But even then there was an unspoken distance between us. I wanted so much to find a woman I could be close to and confide in, but I never found her.

The civil rights movement was in full swing when I was in high school, and although I read about it in the papers, heard about it in school, and saw it on the TV news, I was so wrapped up in my own personal trauma, I couldn't seem to pry myself loose to do something to help. In a way I was fighting my own private civil rights battles. In retrospect, I would have loved to have marched in Birmingham or Montgomery, or to have gone to hear Martin Luther King Jr. speak. I wrote a paper for a civics class in school on the Ku

Klux Klan and realized there were some really evil people in the world. I never understood why or how things had gotten to the point they had, but I felt so far away from it, and so trapped in my own personal oppression, that I just couldn't do anything for the cause.

My father's bigoted and redneck attitudes didn't help any. I had two friends who were sisters—one white and one black—named Colleen and Collette. They had a tough time in school with kids' attitudes and bigotry. In a way, I thought I understood their pain. But my father would not allow me to go to their house. Imagine, an alcoholic pedophile saying I shouldn't go to someone's house because their father was black! There were probably plenty of parents who wouldn't let their kids go to our house either.

One summer night, I went to Lake Shore Park, where they held dances in the pavilion. I was all alone, and so I just walked around, looking for people I knew. I had never gone to one of these dances before. Then I began to notice that mostly black people had gathered there, but at first that didn't mean anything to me. I did notice a sort of tension in the air, but I really couldn't figure out why I felt it. Then I saw Colleen and Collette and walked toward them, hoping to be able to hang out with them. When Colleen saw me, she stuck her elbow out, jabbing me in the ribs, and then yelled at me, "You hit me! Get away from me, you white trash! I'm calling the cops!" At first, I was hurt, and then I was scared to death, because as I looked around, everyone had stopped talking. They assumed I had hit her and they were all staring at me. I didn't know what to do. I was afraid I was going to get beat up! Eventually everyone backed off, and I tiptoed out of the place, my heart pounding in my chest. I walked the whole way home alone, starting to cry once I got away from the park. I didn't understand what had happened. I had thought those girls were my friends. But now, as I look back, I think it was a result of the energy that developed with the civil rights movement.

High school, in general, was difficult for me. When I was in the ninth grade, an advisor who was about ready to retire told me that since I didn't have a mother, and my father was a blue-collar worker, I would probably not go to college. She felt I should take business courses to prepare myself for work after high school. I obligingly did as she suggested and took typing, shorthand, business math, and some other really boring classes. But during the summer between tenth and eleventh grade, it hit me: I really wanted to go to college. I got this crazy idea in my head that I wanted to be a psychologist or even a doctor! So I went to school in the summer and talked to a new advisor (the previous one had retired), begging her to let me into college prep classes. She warned me that if I couldn't keep up my grades, I would be put back into the business classes. I was so excited. I knew if I just applied myself and worked hard, I could make the grade. And I did. I worked very hard, and even though I only got Bs and Cs , I'm not sorry I made the adjustment.

Still, school was so hard. I think I was smart enough to get better grades, but because I couldn't sleep at night, I would sometimes fall asleep in class, and I couldn't concentrate. My mind would wander and it would be as though I was simply somewhere else. As a result, I would miss entire lectures. My face would be red with embarrassment when the teacher called on me to answer a question, and I didn't have even the slightest idea what he was talking about. One teacher gave me the nickname of "Sahara Dry Run" because no answers ever came out of my mouth.

I skipped school all the time because the "demons" would run around in my head. I really thought I was going crazy. I had a hard time making friends in the college prep classes, because most of those kids came from another part of town and I didn't fit in with them. I became somewhat of a loner. I always felt as though I wore a sign that said I was "odd" or "weird" or "queer" or something like that. I must have given off signals that only other people could read. I couldn't see them myself. I know now that kids who are sexually abused do give off signals. They have a difficult time with appropriate boundaries, and sometimes they have a difficult time differentiating between right and wrong. I knew the difference between right and wrong most of the time but where sex and relationships were concerned, I had no clue. I didn't know how to "flirt" with a boy or what was expected of me on a date.

Despite all of this, I graduated from high school in 1966 with my class. I was humiliated, though, at the graduation ceremony. My father showed up drunk, with a married woman with whom he was having an affair. Afterward, when we were all leaving the gymnasium, cheering, happy to be finished with high school, I saw my father get into in a fistfight with the woman's husband, who had apparently followed them and waited for them to come out of the ceremony. Mortified, I just walked in the other direction and pretended I didn't know them. Later that night, my father came home full of bruises with his ribs taped up. I was wishing the guy had killed him!

During high school, I had discovered alcohol. When I started babysitting for an Italian family in our neighborhood, their mother told me to drink warm wine to help with menstrual cramps. I did and it helped. It also did something else. For a short time, I felt like a real person. I relaxed inside just a little, and the demons and nightmares weren't as bad. I could sleep a little bit more during the night if I had had a couple of glasses of wine. But I only did that when I babysat for those people. It never occurred to me to drink my father's beer. However, during my senior year, I learned more about drinking. In Ohio in 1966, you could legally drink beer when you turned eighteen. On my eighteenth birthday, I went to a place called the Beachcomber and had a rite-of-passage kind of evening: I drank beer until I couldn't see straight! In high school I went out a couple of times after that, but not much, considering my father's restrictions. But the summer after I graduated, I got a job at a local shoe store. There, I met a twenty-one-year-old man whose nickname was "Bruiser." He took me to a party where there were people who had graduated from high school two or three years before me. These were more "seasoned" drinkers. Bruiser made me a martini in a Pat O'Brien glass—a huge thing that looked more like a fishbowl! I didn't even know what a martini was at that time. Unfortunately, I loved it. I drank it down, and then went into a complete blackout. When I came out of the blackout, I discovered I was riding in a speedboat out in the lake in the middle of the night. When the boat stopped, Bruiser and I had sex. I was so drunk, I barely remember it. I do know, though, that it was my first act of consensual sex— the first time I did it when I wasn't being raped by my father or uncle. I won't say it was fun; I'm not even sure what I felt. But the next day I felt really awful. I had a hangover, and I felt sick to my stomach when I thought about the sex and whatever else I'd done that I couldn't remember. How could that happen, anyway? When Bruiser came to see me a couple of days later, I told him to go away and to not come back. (However, I didn't tell alcohol to go away.) My boyfriend, Dick never new about this either.

My father had always paid for life insurance policies on us. The insurance man came every month to collect the premiums. He sort of became a friend, stopping in for coffee after dinner and chatting with all of us, as though we were a regular family. My father always told us that when we turned eighteen, the policy would be paid up, and we could choose to keep it or cash it in if we wanted to use it for something important, like buying a house. He didn't mention education, because that wasn't important to him. When I wanted to use it for my first year at Kent State (actually, it would have been enough for the whole four years), my father said to me, "Who do you think you are, some goodie-two-shoes going to college? No one else in our family went to college and we have all done well. But, sure, go ahead and get the money!"

So, after graduation, I enrolled at Kent State University. I was so excited. Except for my mother, who was now deceased, I was the first person in my whole family to graduate from high school or go to college. I decided I could pay for it by cashing in my life insurance policy. But when I arrived at the insurance company and filled out the form to get my money, the woman looked at me with a sad face and said, "I'm so sorry."

"What do you mean?" I replied.

She answered, "Your father borrowed from these policies over the years, and all I can give you is $40.00."

My face turned beet red. I was always embarrassed by him and ashamed to be his daughter. I was so mad at him! It seemed he had broken every promise he ever made. And it also felt like my path was always blocked, no matter what I tried to do. At the last minute, just before classes were to start, my boyfriend, Dick, put me in touch with a ladies' auxiliary group that loaned me the money for the first year's tuition. Dick was in his last year at Kent, and I thought we would get married. In retrospect, I don't think he ever really wanted to marry me. But he did talk about it from time to time, and he even bought me china for my hope chest. In the end, I destroyed the relationship. I had a dream one night that Dick and I were getting married. In the dream I was walking down the aisle toward him, then I looked down and saw that my wedding gown was dirty and torn to pieces.

When I thought about that dream, I decided it meant that I was dirty, that I was damaged goods and I should never marry a good person like him. So I got drunk one night and went out with his best friend, then made sure everyone knew about it. He got mad and broke up with me. (I later learned that he wanted to go back to an old flame, Julie, whom he eventually married.) That was the end. I was incredibly depressed for a long time after that, and cried myself to sleep every night. Thoughts of suicide continued to plague me daily.

Shortly after the first semester at Kent State started, my father insisted that I pay rent now that I had a job. But I couldn't pay rent with my $.95-per-hour job and also go to college at the same time. I thought he should let me live there for free. So to hell with him, I thought. I found a better job at Carlisle's department store and my wages went all the way up to $1.25 per hour. My Friend Becky was working there, and it was great to have more time to spend with her. We spent a lot of time dreaming and fantasizing about things we would do when we got older. She had skills as a graphic artist and worked in the advertising department. We dreamed of being clothing designers and cooked up up a name for our clothing line. We called it "Ronni Jean," a combination of both our middle names. Becky drew a sketch of us in a little car pulling a sailboat on a trailer! What adventures we hoped for!

I moved into a rented room downtown, close to school. It was a relief to be away from my father. I had not fully understood the damage he was doing to me and the incredible tension I was under living with him. I loved being on my own. I went to school during the day and worked at Carlisle's in the evenings. After work, I would go out with friends and drink. This quickly became a serious habit, and eventually a huge problem. I dropped out of school after the second semester, and just worked and drank. At least for the first time in my life, I was getting sleep, albeit alcohol-induced sleep. I still had the nightmares, but I would wake up with relief that I was alone in my own little room. I found out many years later that my friend Lynn refused to tell my father where I had moved to when he asked her. She was a devoted friend. Many years later, I would learn that Dick's mother, Freida, actually helped me to get the room I rented by providing a reference and paying the deposit. I never learned this until well after Freida's death.

Soon after her graduation, Becky went to England with some coworkers from Carlisle's. She had some terrific opportunities, and she jumped at them. Although I was extremely excited for her, I was also a little jealous. I wanted to be going away, too. I knew I would really miss her!

My father had a new woman in his life named Edie. They married shortly after I moved out. I thought this would be good for my little sister, Joyce, but Edie was not the motherly type. I didn't realize until a couple of years later that Joyce was already in trouble with drugs and alcohol. She had started smoking pot and drinking when she was thirteen. I was so naïve about such things that I didn't even know what marijuana was! But she had begun drinking and smoking pot very heavily. She was caught with a bottle of whiskey at school, and was using LSD with friends in the evenings. I didn't learn this until many years later.

After my first airplane ride on a vacation to the Bahamas with Becky, I thought about all those dreams I'd been having about flying. I decided that would be the ultimate escape from everything. I really wanted to fly, to be a pilot. I had no money for flying lessons, and there wasn't even an airport in Ashtabula. So I went downtown to the air force recruiter to sign up. I realized this could be my ticket out of Ashtabula. The United States military was involved in Vietnam, and I figured they would take any warm body that walked through the door. But the recruiter, a fat man sucking on a soggy cigar, sat back in his chair and laughed at me, saying, "Little lady, don't you know girls can't fly in the Air Force? You go get your pilot's license, and then maybe they will let you fly." I was so disappointed. Then I tried to get a job as an airline hostess, as they were called then. I sent an application away to Pan American. I was quickly rejected and told I would be rejected by other airlines as well because, at five feet, I was too short.

So I settled into my job at Carlisle's and decided I would try some other method of getting away from Ashtabula. Drinking became an almost daily part of my life. When I wasn't drinking, I felt like an outcast, with a sign across my forehead that said I was "damaged goods." I had a hard time socializing and being what I considered normal. I couldn't sleep without the nightmares. When I drank, I felt like everybody else, although I don't think I acted like everybody else. My personality changed when I drank and I just got kind of crazy. At least I was able to sleep, though, because I felt nothing when I was drinking. I always knew my father was an alcoholic, and I vowed I would never be like him. I had no idea that I already was an alcoholic. The morning hangovers should have been a warning sign for me, but I thought everyone had these experiences.

I began dating men I met through work and while drinking at St. Angelo's bowling alley, where many young adults hung out. I need to say here that I had no idea what it meant to date. These guys were a little older than me, and they all expected to have sex on dates. I never met anyone else who was like Dick—that is, who wanted to save sex for marriage. I was so confused by the concept of sex and not really sure of anything that I might call morals or values. But I began to think that if I could master sex, that is, learn how to really please a man in bed, he would love me. Warped as that was, it made sense. After all, the only thing close to love I had experienced since age five came from men whose only means of getting close to me was sexual. I had no other frame of reference for sex or love. I had no idea that other people didn't act like this. It would be a long, long time before I learned what my values were.

The problem was, every time I was sexually intimate with a man, it would trigger memories of all those years of sitting on my grandfather's lap, of my uncle raping me, of my father having his way with me. When I saw a penis, it repulsed me. But I couldn't tell anyone about these feelings. I couldn't bear to see a penis or to be penetrated. I actually hated every minute of it, and the only way I could do it was to be drunk. The bottom line was, all I really wanted was to be loved—by anyone.

My nightmares started getting worse. Sometimes I had a dream in which my cervical spine was numb and paralyzed. In the dream a man was about to get on top of me, and I couldn't do anything to stop it. I would actually know it was a dream, and that all I had to do was wake up, but no matter how hard I tried, I could not wake myself up. The fear was paralyzing. I also had dreams of going places and discovering I was completely undressed. Another recurring theme was that I was being chased by police, and I would just lie down, submissively, and let them get me. I thought they would be less likely to hurt me if I was submissive.

When my sister Donna graduated from high school, she joined the navy. She wanted to get away even more than I did. The day after graduation, she went to the recruiter's office and signed up. She told me that when she climbed the steps of the plane to go to boot camp, she looked back and saw herself standing there. She said "Good-bye" and left that Donna and that life behind. She describes it as the most liberating moment of her life.

In the summer of 1968, I went out to San Diego where she was stationed for a two-week vacation. We had a blast going to the beaches every day. I ran into a guy I knew from Ohio, who was stationed in San Diego in the Air Force. He and his friend took Donna and me out and showed us a good time in San Diego. After I got back to Ashtabula, I realized that moving out to California was the way I would be able to leave. I decided I wanted to move out there, get an apartment, and then Donna could leave the base and move in with me. I made a plan to save money and do that as soon as I could. In 1968, the sex, drugs, and rock-and-roll movement was in full swing. And, in California, people became "hippies" and "flower children." That sounded kind of "groovy" to me. It became my plan.

CHAPTER 10

california

In the fall of 1968, I was working hard and saving money for my move to California. Sometime around Thanksgiving week, I ran into John, a man I had met a couple of years earlier. He had moved away from Ashtabula and had become a Los Angeles police officer. He was home on a vacation, and we had a few dates. He didn't ask me to have sex with him, which right away was a good sign to me. He was Lebanese and very tall, dark, and handsome. He seemed to like me. He invited me to move to California and share his two-bedroom apartment. I wanted so much to get away from Ashtabula, but I hadn't saved enough money yet. This seemed like the easier, softer way to get out to California. I could go be a flower child, stay with John, and move to San Diego later. Here was my chance and I took it. I gave a one-week notice to my employer, emptied out my bank account, and packed up all of my earthly belongings, including my sewing machine. Totally unprepared for what lay ahead, I flew out to California and I didn't look back! I moved into John's two-bedroom apartment, occupying his spare bedroom. His roommate had been drafted to Vietnam and left his VW Bug behind, asking John to drive it so it would stay in good condition. So suddenly I had a place to live in California, a car, and a man! Wow! I drove that car for a year without a driver's license, until John discovered it and took me to do my road test. I passed!

I wasn't exactly following my original plan to move to San Diego. But I figured I'd get down there sooner or later, and at least I was in California, away from Ashtabula and far away from my father. I hoped I would never see him or his family again. I had no trouble finding a job through a temporary agency and eventually ended up at Pacific Telephone Company as a long-distance operator.

The interesting thing was that I was as far from being a hippie or a flower child as I could have ever been. Los Angeles policemen were pretty conservative and certainly not hippies. My definition of a *hippie* was someone who rebelled against the establishment by not working, smoking pot, and dressing in clothes that defied all that their parents had tried to teach them. John wasn't like this. I felt like I was with a man whom everyone respected. This couldn't have been further from the truth. Most people hated cops—they called them "pigs." And I would soon learn that cops drank, smoked pot, and even cheated on their wives, too. But still, it was better than what I had come from. I had a new life ahead of me, and I wasn't going back.

I loved California. It rained a lot in the winter, but most of the time the sun was out and everything was green year round. People were not as conservative as they were in Ohio, and there didn't seem to be as many rules to live by. The mountains and the ocean came together and took my breath away. Sometimes we would drive up the coast to San Francisco and stop at all of the Brookside wineries along the way. They had wine-tasting rooms where they would give you little shot glasses of all of the different flavors of wine. By the time we got to San Francisco, we would be drunk. John liked to drink, but I never could figure it out: He could take it or leave it. Even if he got drunk, his personality really didn't change; he just got silly. When I drank, I got drunk and I got mean. I would cry and go into rages about anything.

One night we were entertaining two women who were visiting us from Ohio. I got it in my head that John was spending too much attention to one of them, and I went off the deep end. I cried and carried on—and continued to drink. It seemed the only way to cope with my pain. By this time, John and I were living together as a couple, and even talking about marriage. He told me he was head over heels in love with me and thought I was just wonderful. He liked to call me Jeannie, which was my middle name, and my mother's name. I loved it. But on this evening, I went nuts. I drank so much that I went into a blackout. I was so mad at him that I decided to go out and sleep in the car. Downtown Hollywood, California, isn't a safe place to sleep in your car. Unbeknownst to me, John followed me out to the car. I didn't sleep, but I was in a blackout and don't remember most of it. He tried to talk me into coming back into the apartment, but instead, I began walking down the street. I wasn't even completely dressed. He followed me, and at one point (this I do remember) he kicked me in the butt. I woke up at home, sleeping on the floor, with a terrible hangover. I didn't remember most of what went on the night before, and John was pretty angry. I imagine he was thinking that I wasn't good wife material after all.

That episode was typical of others to follow. And, eventually, John did have affairs with other women. I won't say I deserved it, but then I wasn't much of a partner in a relationship. I had no clue how to be in a relationship. And I still couldn't have sex unless I had alcohol in my system. I wonder why he stayed with me at all.

I never made it to live in an apartment in San Diego with my sister Donna, like I had originally planned. However, I did go down to visit her from time to time. She eventually got married to a marine sergeant named Rich, who was from Maine. When Donna and Rich both got out of the service, they moved to Maine, where his family was, and he became a Maine state trooper. I missed her so much. But I figured she was starting a terrific new life, with a mother-in-law who thought she was the perfect wife for her son. Donna had a new life in a new land with a new husband and a new mother. Wow! Was she lucky!

My job at Pacific Telephone Company was good. I worked as a long-distance operator in Hollywood. This was prior to direct-dial services. You needed the operator to call anywhere outside of your local area, so my job was in demand. I could put in lots of overtime and make extra money. For one whole summer, I worked seven days a week and put the extra money aside for a down payment on a house. John and I found a cute little two-bedroom bungalow in the San Fernando Valley, and we moved in during the fall of 1970. We got a dog and a cat and tried to settle into what seemed like a normal life. I bought a piano and began learning to play with great gusto. On February 6, 1971, the day after my birthday, we got married in a civil ceremony with strangers witnessing, in Las Vegas. The wedding wasn't much to write home about, but we got the honeymoon suite at Caesar's Palace and had dinner show tickets to see the Fifth Dimension. We sat at a table next to Petula Clark! I thought we had really made it to the big time!

But I hadn't yet learned about California earthquakes.

It is the morning after we arrived home from Las Vegas, February 9, 1971, at 6:01 a.m. John and I are getting ready for work, our first day in our home as a married couple. I am standing naked in front of the bathtub, waiting for John to get out so I can get in, when all of a sudden, there is a very loud rumbling. The house is actually vibrating, and I notice my electric rollers and brushes and combs bouncing off the bathroom sink onto the floor. Through the bathroom window, where it is still dark outside, I see bright flashing lights—like lightning, but brighter and several flashes in a row. I am jolted into absolute terror and a bloodcurdling scream emerges from inside me. The roar around us now is so loud, I can't hear my own scream. I look at John, who is just stepping out of the shower and is equally as terrified. As he grabs hold of me and begins to move us toward the door, there is a very loud "bang" and it feels like the house is hit broadside by a fast-moving train. The house begins to move, and we fall in a heap on the floor in the hallway. I hear glass breaking around me and feel water coming down from above. My mind thinks that the roof is gone and it is raining on us. The other thing my mind is telling me, in the longest sixty seconds of my life, is that Los Angeles is being bombed and we will all die from the fallout.

In reality, a 6.5 magnitude earthquake has hit, the epicenter being only a half mile away from us. During the sixty seconds it roared through San Fernando, it uplifted our house, breaking windows, knocking the refrigerator over, sending dishes flying out of cupboards, televisions flying out windows, and my piano walking across the living room. The water I felt on my head was from the toilet, which had been completely pulled loose and the water pipe broken, shooting water up to the ceiling. If you've ever been through an earthquake, you know that the duration is what usually determines the amount of damage. During an earthquake, sixty seconds can cause a great deal of damage.

Our house was badly damaged and the frequent aftershocks just about sent me insane. The dog ran away, never to be seen again, and the cat was found dead under the house. It probably died of fright. I drank beer all day. There were aftershocks that came every fifteen minutes or so for several days following the original earthquake. All of the water, electricity, and sewers were cut off. All of the stores were closed, and many of the streets were now at several elevations, not navigable by car. The house was in such bad shape that we had to leave, and we ended up staying in another city, away from the epicenter of the earthquake, with two bachelor policemen who worked with John. They smoked pot and listened to Janis Joplin on the stereo nonstop. This is when I smoked pot for the first time. The record played over and over all night long. Janis's singing would be in my dreams, and I memorized all of the songs. The pot seemed to help my nerves after the earthquake, but I really didn't like it—I preferred good old alcohol.

CHAPTER 11

the baby

After the earthquake, John announced to me that he had been having an affair prior to our getting married, and that the woman was pregnant. I was devastated. The earthquake had created a new fear in me, and I was afraid to be alone. I didn't want to lose John. The famous case of *Roe v. Wade* had just made abortions legal, and John said the woman would get an abortion if he would pay for it. I suggested he sell his motorcycle and give her the money, and that is what he did. What a great way to start a marriage—by killing a baby! You can bet I got drunk over that one!

When I first became sexually active with John, I started taking birth control pills. Getting pregnant was the last thing I wanted. But after completing the earthquake repairs to the house, John started talking about wanting to have a baby. He said he wanted a "little redheaded Sara" running around the house. Part of me was thrilled that he wanted to do this with me, but the other part of me hated the idea. My childhood had been so awful that I couldn't imagine bringing another child into the world. And I had no clue how to raise a baby. The whole idea scared me to death! But one evening, during a candlelit wine-and-romance evening, after making love John ceremoniously went into the bathroom and flushed all of my birth control pills down the toilet!

The next month, after a camping trip with another policeman and his wife—who made fun of us for staying in the tent so long one morning—I discovered I was pregnant.

I found a good doctor and received prenatal care. I tried to quit smoking—at least I cut down considerably. But I didn't quit drinking. I had no idea that alcohol would harm an unborn baby. I was so preoccupied with being pregnant, getting baby stuff together, and making maternity clothes that I didn't drink as much as I had before. That is, I really didn't get drunk. But I did drink. I didn't know how not to! Still, in terms of my energy and health, I had a wonderful pregnancy.

Unfortunately, the minute my belly started to swell, John wanted no part of me sexually. He kept saying I was fat. My heart was broken. He began sleeping around and was often gone for more than a day at a time with no explanation. Because he was a Los Angeles policeman, whenever he didn't come home, I was always worried he had been shot or killed. He didn't seem to care that I spent nights crying and worrying about where he was. This baby was growing inside of me, and he never once felt the baby move or listened to my belly. He didn't even want me to be close to him in bed, for fear he would feel the baby move. He thought it was creepy. I felt so alone, and so I drank wine when I was home in the evenings by myself.

Around this time I developed a friendship with a man named Charlie. He worked with me at the telephone company, and he was a former Los Angeles policeman. He had resigned after getting shot during the Watts riots. I don't know what the attraction was between us—he was a married man, and I was a pregnant married woman. Still, there was a lot of sexual energy between us, even though we didn't have a sexual relationship. I guess I just needed someone to be close to during my pregnancy. He had a great sense of humor and we laughed a lot. We usually had to sneak out to go places, because we were afraid of people getting the wrong idea about us. I didn't tell John about our relationship, and he didn't tell his wife about me. I guess you could say it was an affair—without the sex. It worked well, though, because John worked the evening shift and I worked days. Charlie worked days, but I guess his wife thought he was working in the evenings we were together. Sometimes we would just drive up to the canyons in his Jeep with a sandwich and watch the sunset. Our friendship continued for a number of years. Being with him made me feel whole and good—and loved. He respected me.

I spent a great deal of time sewing—some for the baby and some to make extra money. I seemed to have a talent for making, and even designing clothes. My friends would hire me to make clothes for them. If you look back in fashion history, the clothing styles in the late sixties and early seventies were changing fast. I would make clothes just like the ones I saw in the stores, only cheaper. I probably didn't charge enough for what I made, but it was good for me to do this. It seemed to be part of the nesting instinct that women have when they're pregnant. I set the money aside so I could take a longer maternity leave from work after the birth of my child.

I also began reading a lot about pregnancy, babies, and motherhood. I remember reading books by Adelle Davis, who was one of the pioneers of the natural food movement during the sixties and seventies. I grew up on food from our garden, so that made sense to me. I bought raw dairy products and fertilized eggs. I ate like a racehorse during my pregnancy, but I only gained about fifteen pounds. I only weighed 119 pounds when I checked into the hospital!

Jennifer Lin, a perfect little girl with a head full of black hair and big brown eyes, was born on December 7, 1972. I guess I wouldn't have that little redhead running around the house like John wanted. Probably John's Lebanese genes were dominant. She didn't, and still doesn't, look anything like me. But she was beautiful and wonderful, and she was healthy and the most beautiful thing that had ever happened to me. It was as though I suddenly had some worth.

At the point in labor when they wheeled me into the delivery room, I suddenly felt my life's priorities make a huge switch. It was as though I had lifted something up to the top and put something else down at the bottom of the pile of "important things." After she was born, I had a new direction in life. I don't know why this didn't happen earlier, when I was pregnant. I certainly felt her life moving inside of me. But life was a mystery to me. I don't think I had a clue what was happening. Oh, physiologically I knew what was happening. But, spiritually, I was dead. Immediately following my daughter's birth, I felt a great sense of relief, because for the first time since I could remember, I didn't want to commit suicide.

I don't know how or why, but I seemed to take to motherhood like a duck to water. I loved every minute of it. But the problem was, I hadn't a clue how to be a good mother. It was easy when Jenni was a baby. I loved her, nurtured her, gave her good nutrition and care, loved her, loved her, and loved her some more. I sat her on my lap on the piano bench and played and sang lullabies to her. I breastfed her until I had to go back to work, when she was about four months old. I hated having to leave her with a babysitter. And, throughout the next few years, the babysitters would be many. It was hard to find a good one, and when I did, something would eventually happen that caused them to quit.

During the first few months after Jenni's birth, John and I were a happy couple again. He loved Jenni and wanted to spend as much time with her as possible. I have a picture of him sleeping on the couch with her, when she was about three months old. She was sleeping on his stomach—precious. But not only did his nasty habits soon return, so did mine. He started staying out at night, and I continued to drink and smoke.

When Jenni was just a year old, I moved out into my own apartment in Burbank. It was awful—bleak and lonely. John would come to visit Jenni once a week and stay for about an hour. He paid me very little child support, and I became a struggling single mom. I dated men and even had an affair with a married man (who actually treated me with more respect than anyone I had ever been with). I continued to drink. Then John and I had a reprieve of sorts, and began to spend nights together again. He wanted me to move back to our house. I wasn't sure. But then I discovered that I was pregnant again. We began talking about getting back together, having another baby, and settling down as a family. I was seriously considering it. Then when I was about eight weeks into the pregnancy, I came down with a life-threatening case of pneumonia. My fever went up to over 105 degrees. I was taking lots of medications, and yet I continued to drink. I decided that all of those drugs, the fever, and the stress might have damaged the unborn baby, so I decided to have an abortion. It was so easy to do—I just walked into a clinic with $130 in cash, filled out a couple of forms, and it was over in a couple of hours—kind of like getting a root canal. But I somehow didn't have the mental or spiritual awareness to fully comprehend exactly what I was doing, and it would be something I would deeply regret for the rest of my life.

After the abortion, I was tired, depressed, broke, and morally beaten up. Thoughts of suicide started to creep into my mind again. I moved back in with John, and we tried to make our marriage work. I even stopped working for a short time, hoping that staying at home would bring our family closer together.

Just before Jenni's third birthday, my sister Joyce, who was twenty-one years old at the time, and was still living in Ashtabula, tried to commit suicide. The doctor said she was in a coma and might not live. She had taken several bottles of narcotics. I took Jenni and flew back to Ohio. Donna and Rich had moved to Maine, and Donna had a baby, Beatrice, who was six months younger than Jenni. We met at my father's house in Ohio and met each other's daughters for the first time. My father was drunk most of the time we were there. Despite my request that he not drink before visiting the hospital for Joyce's sake, he got drunk, went to the hospital, and while she lay there helpless in the hospital bed, he started a senseless argument with her. It really upset me, and after I confronted him about how he was treating Joyce, I went home and told his wife, Edie, who never liked me anyway, that I was going to go stay at the Wheelers' house and that I never wanted to see her or my father again. She gave me a big lecture about what a terrible daughter I was, how I had no respect for my father, and how he could do whatever he wanted. I left.

I stayed with the Wheelers and continued to visit Joyce, who had come out of the coma only to ask why we didn't let her die. I had no skills to talk with her appropriately and no understanding of what she was going through. I saw it as simply a case of her being a drug addict, and because I had never taken drugs, I couldn't relate to her. (Little did I know that being an alcoholic was the same thing!) I didn't understand that Joyce had never been nurtured since our mother's death, that she had simply been "taken care of" by other people, most of whom didn't love her. She was wandering lonely on the earth, probably in more emotional pain than I was. I expected her to have the strength that I had and to just get away and start her own life. But in retrospect, I realize she never really had a chance to develop the skills she needed to accomplish that.

One evening, I met Donna at a local bar. She was begging me to go back to our father's house—she wanted the family to stay together. I was appalled! What family? I explained to her that I only felt a sense of family toward her and Joyce, but not toward my father, and certainly not toward Edie. I told her that being in my father's house gave me the creeps. She didn't understand, so after a few beers, I decided to tell her about the incest. I told her that I hated our father and never wanted to go back there again. She didn't totally understand, but at least she accepted my reason for staying away.

Joyce ended up being sent to a poorly run halfway house outside of Cleveland, the first of many substance abuse treatment facilities she would attend. She was never able to truly conquer her addictions.

I went back to California and tried to resume my life with John. At one point, Joyce came out to live with us. I thought I could straighten her out, but I had no idea what I was getting myself into. I learned—the hard way—that she lied about everything, stole from us, and after we had helped her get an apartment and a job, she then vanished without a word. I learned that she went back to the guy she had been with before she'd tried to kill herself. They stayed in California but moved to Long Beach. I saw her occasionally after that, but I didn't want Jenni around her. Joyce was now into IV heroin use and she hung around with some really scary people.

John and I stayed together for about a year and a half, and then I was hit with another blow. A letter arrived in the mail one day addressed to John from the Los Angeles Department of Welfare. They were asking John if he would provide information about his income and assets. They wanted to know why he wasn't contributing to the support of his daughter, born in September 1991. This was the baby who wasn't supposed to be born! He had paid for an abortion, right after the earthquake.

My mind became so twisted, and my heart was ripped apart. He had been lying to me the whole time. Had he been visiting the baby's mother all this time? Was he having an affair with her? Jenni had a sister! When he came home from work that day, I confronted him with the letter. He pretended he had no idea what it was about—said it was a case of mistaken identity, that it couldn't be him and he didn't want to talk about it. Well, of course, my first coping strategy was to get mad, and the next was to drink—a lot. That was how I coped with just about everything stressful that came into my life.

I ended up leaving John again, but this time I didn't go back. After a long, drawn-out battle between lawyers, we got divorced. I settled for less child support than I was entitled to, but I was afraid to ask for more. John's wallet seemed to be the place he was most sensitive. And I was stubborn; I knew I could make it without him. I considered myself strong and independent. Maybe I was. But I was also a very troubled woman, and unbeknownst to me, I had a long, difficult road still ahead of me.

CHAPTER 12

geographical cure

I moved to Palm Desert—which is right next to Palm Springs—on an invitation from a friend who had moved down there. I loved it—it was hot, dry, and clean. It was a place where people with money bought second homes, so the tax rate was high, making for good schools. I worked as a secretary at Ironwood Country Club, a place in the mountain canyons with golf courses, tennis courts, and expensive second homes. The office I worked in was conveniently located next to the bar, and as a perk for employees, I could have all the beer I wanted. I had found a playground disguised as a job.

At that time I began dating a man named Don. My main attraction to him was that he played the piano—and he did it well. He had studied Chopin for ten years and was an accomplished pianist. He helped me learn more about reading notes and, with a lot of work, I was playing Chopin and Beethoven. But the other big attraction to Don (or drawback, depending on your point of view) was his drinking. We drank together, but he drank more than I did. As a result, however, he would break promises to me and Jenni more times than I could count. Once he showed up at my house so drunk that I wouldn't let him in, and I gave him a little push at the door. He fell down, rolled down the sidewalk, and slept there all night. But I didn't know any better about men, and so I continued to date him. We did a lot of camping and hiking in the canyons around Palm Desert.

One day I got a letter from my father, whom I had not seen since Joyce's attempted suicide. He had bought a motorcycle and was planning to ride across the country. He wanted to visit me. While reading the letter, I began shaking all over. I didn't want to see him again, but I didn't know what to do. I panicked and thought I was losing my mind. Following the advice from a friend, I went to a counseling center. To me, this was an emergency. I was scared to death. I didn't want to see my father, and I certainly didn't want him around my daughter. I felt like my world was falling apart all over again. After an initial evaluation, they assigned me to a female counselor who was quick to pick up on what was going on with me. The first thing she told me was that she had also been a victim of childhood sexual abuse. I was amazed—she looked like she really had her life together! How did she do that? She also told me that I had no obligation whatsoever to let my father come to see me or my daughter. She said that I owed him nothing. This came as an incredible breakthrough for me. I had always felt like I was somehow connected to him and I would never be able to truly get away from him. I also felt that for some reason, children owed something to their parents. This counselor gave me permission to let go of that foolish guilt once and for all.

On my counselor's advice, I sat down and wrote my father a letter, stating that I never wanted to see him again, that what he did to me so long ago was something no one should have to experience, and that the best thing he could do was to stay away from me and go get counseling for himself. I told him that if he came to my house, I would call the police to have him taken away.

He didn't come and I didn't hear back from him. In fact, it would be several years before I would hear from him again. In the meantime, I stayed in counseling. Although sometimes I would arrive for my counseling appointment intoxicated, my drinking was never addressed. In a weird way, I think I wanted the therapist to pick up on it and tell me to stop. But that never happened. One thing that I did accomplish through this therapy was to learn that I wasn't dumb. I always thought I was just plain stupid. But this therapist didn't think that, and to prove it, she gave me an IQ test and the result put me in the "gifted" range (whatever that meant). It was good for me to know this because now I could set some realistic goals for myself. I still wanted to finish college.

I got in a big fight (one of many) with my boyfriend, Don, and we ended up parting ways. After going alone to a party that the two of us had been invited to, and seeing him with someone else, I became extremely depressed. Jenni was up in Los Angeles visiting her father. I couldn't bear to go home alone that night, so I took a bottle of wine and drove up the winding road into the mountains to watch the sunset there. On one of the winding turns, I looked down at my dashboard and noticed I had an empty gas tank. In my drunken stupor, without looking for traffic, I made a U-turn in the middle of the road so I could drive back down the mountain to get gas. I was hit by another car that was behind me. My car almost went off the cliff, and I was saved only by the fact that my tire had been punctured in the collision and stopped me just a few feet away from the edge. I began to cry hysterically, and the people who hit me thought I had been hurt. I think it was then that they noticed the bottle of wine in my car. They put me in their car and drove me back down the mountain to my house. I think they were religious, because on the way down, they talked to me about God. I don't remember exactly what they said, but it seemed to light something, if only briefly, inside of me.

I spent that night alone, crying like a baby. I didn't know where to turn. It seemed my life was falling apart again, and I didn't know what to do. The next morning, my head was a little more clear (except for a pounding headache from a hangover), and I made a phone call to a friend named Bonnie who had recently joined AA. We had been drinking buddies for several years, and although she still lived up in the Los Angeles area, we got together once in a while. She had stopped drinking for three months, and had subtly encouraged me to do the same. I had even gone to an AA meeting with her only a few weeks before the accident, but I decided that I didn't need AA and went to Al-Anon instead. It was through Al-Anon that I learned that alcoholism was a disease, that people didn't mean to do what they did, and that they really had limited choices when they were drinking. I attended Al-Anon meetings for a few weeks, mostly to try to understand my father and to understand Don. It planted a seed in me. So, when I called Bonnie that day, I told her about the accident and that maybe I should quit drinking. She suggested I go to an AA meeting, but my response was "Oh, I don't need to do that. I can do it on my own. This accident has convinced me that I shouldn't drink anymore." She quietly responded, "Well, if you can do it, good for you."

My newfound sobriety lasted less than three days. On the third day without alcohol, I began to shake and sweat and my heart was beating fast. I had no idea that I was in withdrawal. I thought it was just "my nerves" and the stress in my life. Nothing one little glass of wine wouldn't cure. It was only a matter of days before I was back into the thick of my drinking habits.

CHAPTER 13

another geographical cure

My life continued to spiral out of control. I was fired from my coveted job for not getting along with other employees. I got a job with a construction company as a bookkeeper. My boss, the owner, was a loud, controlling man who kept trying to get me into bed. I literally fought him off on a daily basis, much to the amusement of the other employees. I also soon realized that he rarely had enough money to make payroll. One payday there wasn't enough money for any of the paychecks to be cashed. Because I was the bookkeeper and produced all of the paychecks, I was the only one, besides the owner, who knew that the checks would bounce. So I took mine to the bank right away and cashed it, and then I quit with no notice. I had savings that I lived on for a few weeks. After an unsuccessful attempt at reconciling with Don, I made the decision to pack up and move to Maine to be close to my sister Donna. Jenni and I had traveled out there the year before, and I just loved it. I wanted to live there. My decision was made over a glass of wine, as were most of my decisions at that time. I had a garage sale and put a few things in storage. I sadly sold my precious piano. There was no way I could afford to have it moved across the country, only to not have a house to put it in when I got there. It broke my heart, but I resolved I would get another one when I settled in Maine. I sold it to a woman in her fifties who had lost her piano many years ago through a divorce. She had always wanted to be able to play again, so this made me feel a little better about having to lose it. We packed up and I drove my VW Rabbit with Jenni across the country to Maine. Amazingly, I didn't drink any alcohol the whole way.

We camped along the way in the Grand Canyon, the Colorado Mountains, the desert of New Mexico, and the flatlands of Kansas. We stopped in Ohio and visited the Wheelers on our way, but I did not go to see my father. I didn't even drive down the street on which he lived.

We arrived at Donna's house in June 1979. Donna had no idea what was in store for her with me back in her life. I was loud, rude, impulsive, thought I knew it all, and drank a lot of beer. When I arrived at Donna's house, she had gone out and bought a six-pack of beer for me. At first, Donna was thrilled that I had moved to Maine. She and Rich had divorced also, and she was feeling lonely. She had been going to the University of Maine and would start teaching in the fall, something she had always wanted to do. She welcomed us with open arms. But, soon, very soon after we arrived, she would come to wish we had never moved to Maine.

We stayed for a few weeks in an old farmhouse that was on the National Historic Register. It had been built and lived in by a man named Rufus Jones who had been a famous Quaker educator and author of several books about the Quaker way of life back at the turn of the century. It was a very interesting place to live. There were no electric lights in the bedrooms and the beds had straw mattresses. The kitchen had a cooking fireplace and a huge copper cauldron that, in its day, was, I assume, used to wash clothes. There was an attached woodshed with an outhouse that had five holes—two adult-sized and three little ones. I guess in the old days, a family peed and pooped together! In trunks upstairs, there were journals written in pencil by Rufus Jones. They talked about the Quaker philosophy, a way of life I thought I might like, but I didn't know how to get it. While reading it, a little light went on inside of me, that maybe, just maybe, I could have a different life. I had no clue how to get it, though. We had to leave the house when winter came because it wasn't fit to live in during the cold months.

Jenni and I then moved into a little cabin on a lake, just across the road from Donna. Donna and I thought it would be nice if our kids could grow up together. But Donna didn't know how troubled I was, or how much alcohol I drank. She introduced me to a man she had been dating, and I went to bed with him! This type of thing happened on more than one occasion. I don't think I ever really understood how much I hurt my sister during these years, but she seemed to always forgive me and move on. We liked being around for each other, to help watch each others' kids after school and such. For a while, it was good. I found a great job as a field rep. assistant at a labor union—but it should be noted that labor union employees have a reputation of being big drinkers. This place was no exception. I was out of control with my drinking, my behavior, and sexual promiscuity. I had an affair with a married man who drank as much as I did. It was awful. I would wake up in the morning and hate myself for the kind of life I was living, but I didn't know what else to do. I think Donna was really sorry I had moved to Maine and she wanted me to leave although she didn't say so.

I started to think that maybe I was drinking too much. But, I kept saying to myself, I would quit or cut down if my life would just improve. I was a bucket of self-pity—poor me. I thought my life was just terrible when, in fact, I was getting a lot of lucky breaks. I had a wonderful daughter, a decent place to live, a good job, a great car (with payments), and my sister lived right across the road. But still nothing seemed to be going right. My dreams were worse than ever, and no amount of alcohol would stop them from coming.

One night I had a dream that I was cutting my father's head off with an ax, and as his head rolled across the floor, he was yelling my name in a tone he had used all through my childhood. I began drinking through the night and in the morning. I found a listing in the newspaper for the local AA meetings in Augusta, and I cut it out and put it in my wallet. I decided that one of these days I might just go to one.

By this time, I had repressed most of the memories of my childhood, and I could only remember the briefest incidents of incest with my father. When these memories would come back to me, I would drown them with alcohol. I became a miserable person to be around, yelling at everyone. I was terribly mean to my daughter, Jenni. Her reaction to all of this was to start having her own problems. She began having trouble at school, stealing things from the other kids. When the teacher told me about this, I knew that it was my fault, that I wasn't a good mother, and that I didn't know how to give her what she needed. But I lashed out at the teacher and blamed her, telling her to learn better teaching skills.

During the winter of 1979–80, I was thirty-one years old and in very bad shape, emotionally, spiritually, and physically. I couldn't sleep because of the nightmares, and alcohol wouldn't help. I had lost a lot of weight and couldn't eat. I wasn't doing very well at my job. I had reached the point that the only friends I had were people who drank like me. My sister Donna had all but abandoned me and I had no idea why. So I drank to drown the depression. Thoughts of suicide continued to be my relief valve. I knew that if things got too bad, I could cope by killing myself.

Then I saw an ad in the paper for a nanny/housekeeper position for a man whose wife had died. Ralph still had his youngest child at home, a seventeen-year-old girl. He had been stricken with polio in his childhood. Partial paralysis had left him unable to manage his home and farm alone. I somehow thought this was a *"calling"* to me, and so I packed up my things and my daughter and moved in with him. It turned out to be the beginning of another nightmare.

He drank more than I did, and he had seizures when he drank. He was mean and abusive and yelled more than I did. (He reminded me somewhat of my father.) My daughter was afraid of him, but I just thought he needed to be loved and he would be okay. It was far more complicated than that.

One day, he told me that I was a "bitch" when I drank and that I should stop drinking altogether. I didn't let him know that I had actually thought about it several times but I secretly made a phone call to a woman named Geri from AA. I told her I wanted to cut down on my drinking. She was very nice and didn't seem to judge me. She lived nearby and said she would take me to an AA meeting, and we set up a date for the following Thursday to meet. I never made it to that meeting with her; instead I got drunk. That night was the night I left Ralph's house.

There was a terrible thunder and lightning storm going on, and a tree had fallen in the driveway. Ralph and I were both drinking, and he was in pretty bad shape. He fell on the floor and had a grand mal seizure. I just stood there, doing nothing—I had no idea how to help him. My daughter was standing across the room in her pajamas, wide-eyed, looking at me for answers. Something was telling me I need to get her out of there, and to do it immediately! I throw a few clothes and belongings in the back of our car, and in the midst of the thunder and lightning, I drove over the lawn and around the fallen tree, only to find Ralph standing at the end of the driveway trying to block my way.

I was completely scared out of my wits, and I yelled to him, "If you don't move, I will run over you!" I was moving the car toward him, and just in the nick of time, his daughter, Kelley, came along and pulled him to safety. I roared out of the place, not looking back. I looked over at Jenni who was sitting in the passenger seat crying. I tried to console her while driving, under the influence, back to my sister's house, thirty-five miles away. Although I didn't understand it then, I now believe that angels carried us safely through that storm to my sister's house.

Donna took us in—again. I guess she was just glad we were safe. I think she must have thought I was crazy—I know I thought I was.

I couldn't get back into my little cabin; it had been rented to someone else. So I moved into an old, drafty farmhouse that was owned by an elderly woman whose husband had died. She had gradually lost her sight and had to go into a nursing home. Her son, who lived in New York, needed someone to housesit until spring, at which time he would sell the house. It was kind of a neat old house, filled with antiques. I believe there was even a ghost in one of the upstairs bedrooms!

We spent Christmas 1980 there. On Christmas Eve, I invited some friends over for drinks. There was an awful snowstorm, and the temperature went to below zero, so they didn't come over. I had bought every conceivable type of alcoholic beverage known to man in an effort to please them, in hopes they would like me better. I had no other frame of reference to make friends. These people actually didn't drink very much anyway. Then, when they didn't' come, I drank most of the booze myself. I was so depressed that I cried myself to sleep after putting the presents from Santa under the tree. It was a cold, cold wintry night. The old house was heated primarily by a kerosene heater in the kitchen. Sometime during the night, the kerosene jets became plugged with soot, and the flame went out, causing kerosene fumes to be sent into the house, a potentially lethal situation. Below zero temperatures outside caused the house to cool down quickly. Jenni was asleep in her bed, and I was "passed out" in my own and didn't notice what was happening. Another "angel" would come to our rescue that night.

Tiger, the cat that had come with the house, began pacing on my bed, back and forth, meowing and crying and pawing at my face until I woke up. I noticed right away that the house was very cold, and when I got up I immediately smelled the gas. I was able to get the gas turned off and let in some fresh air. I built a fire in the fireplace to warm the house up and I stayed awake until morning. If it hadn't been for that cat, Tiger, we would have either been asphyxiated or frozen to death on Christmas Eve. I was dumbfounded. I knew something big had just happened, but I really didn't understand the whole thing. Somewhere in the back of my mind, I knew it had something to do with my drinking, but I seemed to lack the wherewithal to figure it out. I'm a smart person, but unbeknownst to me, my brain had been hijacked! I wasn't functioning on all four cylinders.

We ended up moving out of that house and back into the cabin by the lake shortly after Christmas, where, in January 1981, my world would be changed forever.

CHAPTER 14

i saw the light

One evening, shortly after moving back into the cabin, I was having one of my regular nights—that is, I was drinking, crying, and feeling sorry for myself. I had reached the point that I couldn't go anywhere except for work, because I was so paranoid. My last visit to the grocery store, about two weeks before, had ended with me leaving a cart full of groceries and running out of the store after hearing what clearly sounded like my father's voice in the next aisle (they call this behavior auditory hallucinations). These things had begun to happen a lot, and I didn't know what to do about them. I was afraid that if I told someone, they would send me to a psychiatric unit where I would be labeled schizophrenic, then medicated and forgotten. My only contact at this time was with my sister and her friend, George, and people through work, even though I called in sick often. They were getting tired of me, too. My daughter was having a hard time in school and she didn't sleep well at night, sometimes walking and talking in her sleep. Her behavior was growing erratic, and I knew it was my fault, but I didn't know what to do about it.

One cold, snowy night in January, when all I could think about was suicide, I called a crisis hotline. A recording answered. I don't even recall what it said because I threw the phone across the room. How stupid to put a recording on a suicide hotline for people who want to kill themselves! I put on my coat, thrust my sweaty bare feet into boots, and began walking down the road in a snowstorm. I was very intoxicated, and I was hoping I would just pass out in a snow bank and they would find me in the morning, dead. Instead, I ended up at a country store where, tearfully, I called my sister. (It took many attempts because of my inebriation.) George came and picked me up. I don't know what he thought, but he didn't say much. He just asked if I would be okay and then dropped me off at my home.

I drank that night until I passed out. (Jenni was staying overnight at a friend's house.)

The next night, the weather was pretty much the same. Jenni was sleeping in her bedroom, and I was drinking wine and listening to sad songs on the record player. One song I played over and over kept talking about loving yourself and finding your strength in love. It said that if you find yourself in a lonely place, you should find your strength in love—love for yourself. When I realized exactly what it meant, I realized that I *didn't* love myself—not one little bit. I thought I was a horrid piece of trash, stupid, damaged goods, worthless, and hopeless—just plain no good. And there didn't seem to be any hope for anything different. I didn't know what love was. I felt as though I had been trying as hard as I could to make a good life, but it wasn't working. I was as far away from my dreams as I could possibly be. When I looked in the mirror, I did not see the woman I hoped I would be at that age. I was so incredibly unhappy. I felt like I was in a deep, dark hole with no light visible at the top. I couldn't figure out how other people did it. Why did they smile? How did they stay happy? I didn't know.

Although I loved my daughter, Jenni, more than any other living creature in the world, I figured she would be better off living with a pack of wolves than with me. I decided right then to commit suicide. I was so self-absorbed that it didn't occur to me to think about Jenni getting up in the morning to an empty, cold house with Mommy just gone. It didn't occur to me how scared she might be—that she wouldn't have a mom (just like me), and that this would cause lifelong damage and harm to her. My inability to think about those things was quite possibly due to the amount of alcohol in my brain, combined with my extremely depressed, hopeless state of mind. All I could think about was myself.

My plan was to get in my Volkswagen Rabbit and, without putting my seatbelt on, drive as fast as I could. When I saw an eighteen-wheeler barreling toward me (which there were plenty of on our road), I would simply move over to the wrong side of the road, allowing the truck to hit me head-on. I figured the impact would kill me, but not the driver of the truck. And if it only maimed me for life, it would be no worse than the nightmare I was living in now. Again, I didn't consider the pain, anguish, and possible injury to the truck driver.

I put my coat on and tiptoed into Jenni's room to see her one last time. Then I decided to have one more glass of wine "for the road." While drinking it, I listened to my sad records again. I heard that same song, the one about loving yourself, and I looked up at the ceiling and said, with slurred speech, tears streaming down my cheeks, "I don't love myself, and no one else loves me, either. And God, if You're there, I don't even love You! Where have You been all my life anyway? Why should I love You?" I didn't know how to turn to God with my fears and loneliness. I only pushed Him away.

At that very moment, something incredible happened that to this day, I cannot explain. It seemed like the little cabin filled with light—I mean, bright light—like a million sunrises. Instead of scaring me, it caused me to feel warm all over and, if only for a moment, to see things clearly for the first time in my life. It was as though a laser beam had penetrated my alcohol-soaked brain and allowed me to see exactly what was happening—for possibly the first time in my life. As this was happening, I looked at the glass of wine I was drinking and realized that it was the alcohol that was killing me. I also somehow realized that if I stopped drinking, maybe I could straighten my life out.

Well, the bright light subsided, the record player continued playing, and I realized I was still drinking the wine. It was like my arm was on autopilot. I couldn't stop, even though I now knew I absolutely had to. The words on the record sang, "The big parade is passing, — what good is living in a world you'll never know." I couldn't figure this out. I began to cry—not the usual "beer tears," but really cry from my gut, belly sobbing. I don't think I had cried like that since my mother died in 1954—a long time ago. Through the tears and sobbing, I remembered that I had the AA meeting list in my wallet. I took it out and looked at it. There was a meeting the next night in Augusta, and I decided I would attend. But I had to find someone to take care of Jenni. I called my sister Donna and asked her if she would watch Jenni the next night so I could go to the AA meeting. I was so intoxicated on the phone—it should have been obvious. But Donna said, "You don't need to go to an AA meeting. You're not an alcoholic—you just want to get attention." She eventually did agree to watch Jenni. I was shaking all over after our conversation, and I drank all of the wine and passed out that night. I got up the next morning with my usual hangover, but something was different. I went to work. I didn't' tell anyone what was going on, but my coworkers kept asking me if I was alright—they thought I seemed somehow weird or different. I said I was fine. The truth was, I was far from fine. But I finally had an idea of which of life's many paths to take—and I was hell-bent to take the right path, no matter how difficult it would be. Still, I wasn't going to tell these people about it—they were the ones who had bottles of Jack Daniels on their desks!

I didn't drink any alcohol that day, and I did go to the AA meeting that night. I really thought I was going there to learn how to just cut down on drinking. But after listening to people talk, I realized that I, too, was an alcoholic, just like they were. The only thing I could do was to quit completely. They all did it, so why couldn't I? I picked up a white chip that night. I was told that, if I felt like drinking, I should put the chip in my mouth, and when it melted, then I could drink! Actually, the white chip meant a lot to me. It meant I had joined life. I was on the train, going somewhere—finally. This all felt so right! But I was also scared to death. I had no idea what I was getting into.

I went to a meeting every night, and went out for coffee after the meetings with people who actually invited me. I couldn't believe it. These people didn't know me, but they invited me to go out with them! Would they dump me once they got to know me? Everyone else had. After two days, I was in full withdrawal from alcohol, although I didn't know it. I began shaking uncontrollably, and my head was pounding and spinning at the same time. I couldn't sleep and I couldn't eat. All I did was drink coffee and smoke cigarettes. I went to work, but I did such a poor job that my work all had to be redone. After a meeting on the third night, a woman who was loud and sarcastic like me, named Libby, sat and told me that I should be in a hospital during my detox. I thought she was nuts and told her I would be okay. She gave me her phone number and said I could call anytime and she would help me. What I didn't know at the time was that I was hallucinating and talking gibberish. The next day, at work, I really thought I was going nuts. I couldn't concentrate; I couldn't even talk straight. I was in tears most of the time and didn't know why. I called my new friend Libby and told her what was going on. She said again that I should be in a hospital, and this time I agreed. I went to my boss and told him the truth about what was happening. It turned out that his wife was an alcoholic and he had been to Al-Anon. He was very supportive and told me my job would be waiting when I came back. I had plenty of vacation time (I had used up all of my sick time), and I had disability insurance. So my paycheck would continue. (Those angels at work again!)

I went to visit Donna's friend George. In hindsight, I know that I wasn't a good judge of character, especially when it came to men. But somehow I instinctively knew that George was a good person, and I trusted him. (I think he was another angel.) He had been saying that he wanted to move out to live in a cabin on the same lake where I was living. So when I went to see him, I suggested he could try it out for a month, and I asked if he would come and stay at my house and take care of Jenni while I went into an alcoholism treatment program. He wasn't totally surprised. I mean, after all, he had picked me up a few nights before at the country store, drunk! And it wasn't the first time he had seen me drunk. I also found out that his brother-in-law was a recovering alcoholic and was now a counselor out in Minneapolis. Sensing my need to have an immediate answer, he quickly agreed to help me, and asked how soon he needed to go out to my house. I asked him to come that night, since in my state of withdrawal, I was getting scared and didn't want to be alone. He came. He stayed with Jenni. He was terrific!

On my thirty-third birthday, I entered a twenty-eight-day treatment program at Eastern Maine Medical Center in Bangor called The Alcohol Institute. The program was an incredible experience. Libby told me that I would have a screening with Dr. Evans. She said that if I didn't pass the screening, I wouldn't get in. I was still kind of smug, and I figured I could get through this interview. I wanted them to take me because I was afraid of what might happen to me if I was left to my own devices. My brain seemed to be on a new wavelength and I couldn't figure it out. I needed help. I thought I had to talk them into taking me. Things couldn't have been further from the truth.

The screening was with Dr. Evans who was, I believe, the first black man I had seen in Maine. He was very intense and somewhat intimidating. The screening was actually with his whole treatment team, at a conference table with people throwing questions at me from every direction. This was very difficult for me, because I didn't know how to behave in a room full of people. I didn't know who I was, as I had spent my life acting out different parts, each part dependent on whom I was interacting with. I was a mess. I can only remember one question that was asked of me, and it threw me for a loop. They wanted to know about my family and if they would be attending the family sessions at the hospital. I told them my sister would, but not my father. Dr. Evans looked at me with angry eyes and said, "Why don't you want your father there? We don't treat people here if they won't allow their family members to be part of the treatment." I was terror-stricken. There was no way I was letting my father become a part of this phase of my life, or any other part of my life for that matter. Why should that be a requirement? Still believing the incest was my fault, I did not tell them about my father. But I was terrified they wouldn't let me in. Then they said the interview was over and for me to go down to the main lobby and wait for their decision.

Shaking and crying, I went with Libby down to the first floor and sat there. She told me that she had overheard them saying they had no beds, but that they didn't want to let me go home so they were going try to get me in somehow. About that time, a disheveled man came walking through the lobby with a poorly packed suitcase, clothes spilling out the sides. He went to the payphone in the lobby, and while looking in his pocket for a dime to make the call, he dropped a white plastic poker chip on the floor. As he began making his phone call, Libby turned to me, pointed to him, and said, "There's your bed!"

She was right. About fifteen minutes later, someone came down and told me to go out to the car and get my suitcase. I was staying.

I felt weak all over. I had been rescued from the brink of death. On my way back into the hospital with my suitcase, I had a vision of a lamb about to fall over a cliff, and an angel rescuing the lamb just in time. I stopped and put the suitcase down. I told Libby about it and said, "That lamb is me, isn't it?" Libby smiled. She knew. She had been there, too. I don't think my feet touched the ground all the way into the hospital. It felt like someone or something was carrying me. I guess "someone" had been carrying me for a long, long time.

I need to stop here and say a few words. This isn't hocus-pocus. Everything I'm saying is true—at least it is my truth. I'm not making anything up. The fact is, alcohol destroys your brain, your body, your soul, your spirit, your intellect, your family, and your life. It slowly sucks the life right out of you and leaves you empty. And it takes nothing short of a miracle to get your life back. In my case, it took several miracles.

As much as I wanted this treatment, it wasn't easy for me. And I didn't make it easy for the clinicians who were there to help me. My mistrusting personality and my lack of boundaries and personal values caused a lot of eye-rolling and disgusted sighs. I made them earn their money. Not intentionally—I just didn't know any better. As I look back on it, I don't know how I ever managed to keep a job all those years. And I really don't know how anyone let me be a mother.

The treatment program was mostly based on group therapy. There were about thirty patients there, and we were divided up into three groups. Sometimes we were divided into two groups by gender. I learned that it was called the Johnson Model, after a man named Vernon Johnson from Minneapolis who developed the treatment. It combined the twelve steps of AA with clinical therapy models. There were classes, videos, group therapy, lectures on spirituality, art therapy, and some individual therapy. We had a lot of homework, which consisted of writing about all the stuff we had done while drinking. What I learned was that addiction is incurable. It only keeps getting worse, and it is potentially fatal if not arrested. I learned that the effects are mental, spiritual, and physical. And fixing it is not as simple as fixing a broken arm or suturing a cut to the skin. This went below the skin, deep inside, where I had never ventured before. It was soul-searching. How do you search your soul if you don't know if you even have one?

My counselor's name was Bobbi, and she had a lot of patience with me. Most of the time, I didn't have a clue what the therapists were talking about. But their method of repetition worked. After hearing the same thing for three weeks, some of the stuff began to soak into my brain. Dr. Evans would hold a big meeting for the whole bunch of us two or three times a week. I dreaded these meetings, because he had a big stick—one of those pointers that teachers use. He would thwap it on a table to get our attention and then he would pick on people and ask what seemed like awful questions. He scared me to death and I had no answers for his questions. He usually asked me why I was so angry. The truth was, I didn't even know I was angry, let alone why. I knew I was hurting. Not physically. I was hurting inside—in my heart. I didn't think I could make it through. I had always been able to work through things in my life—I thought I was tough. But this, I didn't understand. I knew I needed the treatment, but I was having trouble. I thought they would kick me out. And every day I would think about suicide. It was the only thought process that worked for me when I reached a certain point. I was so empty inside that the pain was sometimes just unbearable. However, in AA I had learned the concept of taking things one day at a time. So each time suicide came into my mind, I would say to myself, *Not today. If it's this bad tomorrow, I'll do it.* But then tomorrow would come, and I would say the same thing. It worked. But I was afraid twenty-four hours a day. Someone said, "Don't let your fear stop you—don't be afraid of your fear!" I heard that, and I developed a mantra: "I can function while being afraid." I would say it to myself every time I found I was scared.

Saturday was family day. They would seat everyone—all of the patients and all of their family members—in a big circle in a large room. It amounted to about 150 people. Then they would put each patient in the hot seat in the center of the circle, place the family members in front of them, and the family would proceed to tell the patient how awful they had been. It was like a three-ring circus! So much for confidentiality. All your dirty laundry, your worst secrets, the most terrible things you had ever done, were flaunted in front of 150 strangers! It was like a public torture chamber. A public flogging would have been easier. So each week, I had Saturday to look forward to! One of the Saturdays was devoted to my family. My sister Donna came with my daughter. For some reason, they put us alone in a small room. I was so relieved. I don't think I could have done it in that circle. Donna stated that she didn't like the way things had been going since I had arrived from California and she didn't like the way I took care of Jenni. But she also said she thought I was strong enough to get through this, and she even said that she didn't think she could ever do what I was doing. Coached by a counselor, Jenni told me that she had been pouring my wine down the drain when I wasn't looking! I had no idea. She was scared to death, and she didn't say much else. But it helped me to realize that the impact of my drinking affected people in ways I was unaware of. At the end of the session, I had the opportunity to say something. I tried hard not to cry, because it seemed that was all I was doing lately. But I was able to tell Donna how much I appreciated her help and her being here for me. And I was able to tell Jenni that I loved her more than anything in the world and how sorry I was that I had put her through this nightmare. I assured her I was going to get better. Painful as all of this was, it was so important for the people I had hurt to have the space to talk and for me to tell them I was sorry. The enlightenment I felt from this process helped me to focus my treatment better and move on in my recovery.

While in treatment, I learned that people with alcoholism or drug addiction eventually start living against their value system. It took me awhile to understand this concept, because, the truth was, I didn't even know what my value system was! I didn't know what values were. The values I was taught in childhood weren't anything I wanted to live by. It was almost as though I didn't know right from wrong. And I had developed a habit of lying all the time—even when the truth would have been easier. I started to cover up things I had done while drinking. Then I would make up stories, not remembering the truth because I had been in a blackout. I would lie about how much I had been drinking. The habit of lies just grew until I wasn't sure if I ever told the truth. But I hadn't been aware of it. These were not my birthright values, but I didn't know that. I would have to work hard to learn them. In the meantime, to keep myself in a safe place I borrowed other people's values. That is, I listened to people whom I believed to have a relatively solid value system and just decided those would be my values for the time being. This included things like not lying, not cheating on my income taxes, paying my bills on time, not stealing, and not going to bed with men. As I began to think about those "borrowed" values, I felt a little more grounded and ready to move on in my recovery. It felt odd, like wearing someone else's clothes, but it worked. It kept me safe.

Somewhere along the line, someone told me about a Native American tale about honesty and conscience. According to the story, everyone has a piece of tin situated inside his belly, just under the rib cage, that is shaped like a triangle, with very sharp edges. When a person tells a lie, the tin triangle tips forward, causing a sharp pain in the gut. The only way to relieve the pain is to tell the truth. To extend the lesson to alcoholics, it was said that not only does the alcohol numb the pain, but the corners of the triangle begin to soften and become rounded, so there is very little pain when telling a lie. When you get sober, it takes hard work and practice to begin telling the truth again. I loved this story. I understood that pain in the gut completely! It helped me to shape my own values.

I had no understanding of sexual values. Where would I have gotten these values from? I had no idea when there was sexual energy between me and someone else, and I didn't know that I could say "no" to sex. All I ever wanted was to be loved. All I ever got was being taken advantage of by men who just wanted to get laid. Every time I was with a man, I could only have sex while intoxicated, mostly because I couldn't stand the whole process. I hated the sight of a penis and didn't want to touch it. I couldn't have sex sober.

My concept of sex and love was this: I thought you had to try hard to please a man in order to be loved. I couldn't have been further from the truth. And with each experience, my self-worth was chipped

Sara Orbeton

away until I had none left. And each time, the rape experiences of my childhood would be relived, over and over and over again. I felt like a non-person.

I truly believed that if I were walking down a sidewalk and I saw another person coming toward me, I would not have the right to stay on the sidewalk. I felt I should move over to the grass and let them pass by. But my behavior didn't always reflect this. I saw other people who thought highly of themselves and I would try to imitate them. The end result was arrogance and self-righteous behavior.

I had no idea what it meant to be happy. I would see people laugh, so I would laugh, too, but I didn't know what we were laughing about. Inside, I was crying. I had no personal identity. I didn't know who I was. If I had been asked to describe my personality, I couldn't have done it. In treatment I slowly came to realize that most of my life I simply imitated people. If I was with someone who had a Southern accent, before too long I would be talking with a Southern accent. I would try to laugh the way that person laughed. The way I saw it was, these people were accepted in the world and if I acted like them, I, too, would be accepted. So, whomever I was with, I would imitate. This is why it was so difficult for me to be with a group of people. I didn't know which person to imitate! So the group time in the treatment program was excruciating for me. But at the time I didn't understand why.

"I can function while being afraid."

I once saw a movie starring Jodi Foster about a girl who had been kept in a basement room, away from all people, even sunlight, her whole twelve years. She was like a little wild animal when they found her, and she couldn't interact with anyone. She knew how to speak English, but she didn't know how to use the language properly. She didn't' know how to trust people; she had no boundaries but was highly defensive. When I saw that movie, I knew exactly how that girl felt.

After a month, it was time to leave The Alcohol Institute. I was scared but I had a fist full of new tools to use to stay sober and begin my long road to recovery and a new life. I felt like Dorothy in *The*

Wizard of Oz when the house lands and suddenly everything is in color! But at the same time I didn't know where I was. It was as though I was in a new country having to learn a new culture and a new language. Where was that yellow brick road when I needed it?

I had called my friend Libby to ask if she would pick me up when it was time to go home. Her response was, "Yeah, if I'm not drunk!" This really scared me, because she reportedly had had five years of sobriety. If it was truly that difficult to stay sober, I was in for a long, difficult life. And I really didn't know if she would pick me up. I wondered if I would have to take a bus the seventy-five miles back home. I later learned that this response might not have been the best response for her to give. That is not how I practice my sobriety. Nonetheless, Libby was the person (angel) who was responsible for getting me into treatment, and for that I am eternally grateful.

CHAPTER 15

a new life begins

When I returned to my little cabin, I saw about a dozen yellow bows tied to the trees. I knew my sister had done this, and with tears in my eyes I slowly walked into the cabin with hope for a renewed relationship with her. I now would begin my new life. It was springtime, with flowers blooming and longer days. It was incredible. I actually thought I could hear the leaves opening up on the trees! Each sunrise was a miracle. I kept looking around and seeing so much for the first time.

I went back to work, only to discover that it was not a safe place for me to be. My fellow employees tried to be supportive, each one coming into my office and giving me a reason why he or she had cut down on drinking. One person said he was on the Atkins Diet, which didn't allow alcohol, at least not a lot. Another person said he had been to the doctor and was diagnosed with high blood pressure, and so he had to cut down on alcohol. On and on it went. But the truth was, none of them actually *quit*. I realized that my complete abstinence and having addressed my alcoholism so aggressively made them extremely uncomfortable, so they were responding to their discomfort with their stories. I actually appreciated that they cared. But I couldn't continue to work there. Not only did everyone drink, but the political environment didn't fit with my newfound values.

With a recommendation from my primary care physician, I quit. However, the unemployment office didn't think this was adequate for me to collect unemployment benefits. So I was suddenly broke. I appealed the decision, but it took months. In the meantime, I conducted an aggressive job search. I had never in my life had trouble finding a job, but I soon realized that no one wanted to hire someone who told them she was a recovering alcoholic. Although I was learning how to be rigorously honest for the first time in my life, I really didn't know the ropes. I became uncomfortable in interviews when telling the truth, and I soon learned the interviewers didn't need to know *everything*. I was giving too much information. (I think the don't-ask-don't-tell rule should have been in effect.)

I was too proud or stubborn (or stupid) to go to the state and collect welfare. So I cleaned houses, mowed lawns, and did sewing for people—anything that would earn a buck. My friend George had moved into the cabin next to me and together we grew a garden. I caught fish from the little lake I lived on, and we basically had a back-to-the-earth kind of summer. It was a difficult but positive experience. I gathered huge rocks from the lake (something I later learned was illegal) and built a lovely stone walk up to my cabin. This repetitive, physical labor was therapeutic for me. It gave me time to reflect and feel useful at the same time. The perspiration helped to further detoxify my body and soul from the physiological and spiritual poisons I had ingested over the years. I highly recommend physical labor for anyone who needs a time of soul searching. Splitting and stacking firewood is as good as stonework.

While in treatment, I learned that building sobriety is much like building a house. You have to start with a good foundation, made of good materials and quality construction. Sobriety's foundation is spirituality—and a belief in a higher power. Without it, you will only have what they call white-knuckle sobriety. It took three weeks of repetition of the spirituality lecture in the hospital for me to really get what they were talking about. But I remember when it happened for me—it was as though a cloud lifted and the sun was behind it. I understood what they were talking about. My problem was, I had no idea who or what God really was. And, the night I became aware of my alcoholism, I had loudly professed that I hated God. At this point, I didn't know how I felt. My concept of God was a mixture of some bearded man sitting on a throne making everyone feel guilty, and my mother with angel wings flying around keeping an eye on me. I had never truly prayed. Oh, I always bowed my head when everyone said the Lord's Prayer, but I wasn't sincere. I didn't know what it was all about. However, I had received the message loud and clear that if I didn't soon figure it out, I wouldn't be able to stay sober. For me, that meant not staying alive. I asked people in AA about it, and they said things like "Oh, don't worry about the God stuff—just keep coming to meetings." But I knew I had to get the God stuff.

It was suggested to me that I go down to the river and watch the flow of the water and try to get in touch with the power that made the water move. I did. It was really awesome. The Kennebec River in Augusta was a large, tidal river and it sometimes had quite a fast-moving flow. The waves in the ocean had the same effect to me. I always knew I loved the ocean with its big waves and powerful tides, but I never tied it to a higher power. But when I started thinking about it, I realized that it didn't really matter if I knew, scientifically, what made it all work. The fact was, it was an incredible power greater than human power.

I remember someone at an AA meeting asking me why we needed to have a higher power. (Why would they ask me?) After thinking about it for a minute, I said, "I realized that my alcoholism is a powerful, incurable disease. It is much more powerful than me. In order to overcome this disease, I needed to enlist a power greater than my disease." After saying that, I realized that I had just figured that out while saying it! Now I understood! And it wasn't just about fighting the urge to drink. Actually, I never had the urge to drink, not once, after I quit. My problem was all the demons coming up in my head that wouldn't go away, and I needed all the help I could get to keep from going completely crazy and/or committing suicide.

Early in my sobriety, an image began forming in my head. It wasn't a dream, just a mental image of what my sobriety looked like from the inside. The image was of me in a cage, like a bird. The door was unlocked, but not yet opened. My arms, like wings, had been tied behind me for fifteen years, and they were now free. But they hurt and stayed behind me for a long time. This image would change as time went by, to the cage door opening, my arms beginning to limber up, and me finally flying out of the cage. The cage was my alcoholism, and it had kept me a prisoner for the fifteen years I had been drinking, since my eighteenth birthday. I had also been a prisoner of my father's alcoholism. I was now setting myself free. If only I'd known sooner that I had the key to unlock the door!

Following my residential treatment, I was referred to an agency in Augusta called New Directions for what they called aftercare. I thought "New Directions" sounded good. I certainly needed some new directions! The old ones hadn't gotten me anywhere! I was assigned to a counselor named Barbara, whom I would later learn was one of my many angels. (I think she was the angel supervisor!) My first appointment with Barbara occurred about a week after I got out of treatment. The first thing she did when I sat down in her office was to ask me if I smoked. I said that I did, thinking I would get the lecture that there is no smoking in the building and that I should quit because it was bad for my health. Instead, a grin spread across her face, she opened up her desk drawer and pulled out an ashtray, and we lit up! I remember a little tugging inside of me that said this was going against my newfound values of following rules and being honest. But I didn't put the cigarette out. And it seemed to open up a level of trust with Barbara, important for ongoing treatment.

After a few individual sessions with Barbara, I entered a therapy group of all women, which she co-facilitated. This is where the work really began. I saw my life as a journey—like a path or a road. This part of the journey would be very long and winding, with a lot of tough mountains to climb, large ravines to cross, places where it would be so dark you couldn't tell which way to turn. But I learned that when it was dark, I couldn't just stop, because then I would never get to the rest of the journey. I couldn't just stand at the bottom of the mountain, either, because then I would never make it to the other side. I learned to literally put one foot in front of the other and keep going, no matter how tough it was. I also learned that I didn't have to do this alone. This is what the people in AA were for, what the women in the group were for, and what the angels were for, and of course this was why I needed a higher power. There are times when we're completely alone on our path, and yet we really aren't alone—that higher power is always there. This was a completely new concept for me—and I liked it.

They say that you have a sort of honeymoon period of sobriety that's called the *"pink cloud."* I fell off my pink cloud when I entered this therapy group. Hard. I slid into a deeper depression than I had ever been in, and the suicidal thoughts came back with a vengeance. All of the fear, rage, and anger that had been boiling inside me since I was a little girl was still there and had begun to build a head of steam. I was no longer cooling it down with alcohol. The fifteen years of repressed memories were percolating to the surface of my brain at a frightening speed. When I entered treatment, the only part of it all that I remembered was that my father had made me go to bed with him a few times. All the rest I had blocked. Now I was remembering. The memories were haunting me, getting into my dreams, or nightmares, and making me even more crazy than I had been before. The group therapy was like a double-edged sword—talking about it made it more real, but the pain was there, still waiting for me.

"I can function while being afraid."

One of the subjects that frequently came up in group was the concept of self-worth. I began to realize that not only did I have little or no self-worth, but I didn't even know what it was. Did other people have it? Wow. The more we talked about it, the more I believed I was such a piece of damaged goods that I couldn't seem to conjure up any self-worth. Then Barbara told me something—actually she had to say it several times for me to hear it. She said that everyone— every person on this earth, rich, poor, good, bad, evil, smart, dumb, blind, deaf, everyone—is born with one unit of self-worth. No more, no less. If she was right, that meant I was worth just as much as everyone in the group—worth as much as Barbara, worth as much as, well, everyone! How could that be? Why then were they entitled to be happy, and I wasn't? Did everyone have the nightmares I had? No, they didn't. That, I learned, had nothing to do with self-worth. I had self-worth—one unit, to be exact. But my belief of my worth was poisoned by all the things that had happened to me in my life. It would be tough going to turn that around.

My depression was so deep that I don't know how I went on each day. I did my best to put on a smile when I could with Jenni. I would smile at her in the morning when inside I was in pain and only wanted to cry. I would go outside for walks in the woods or out in our little aluminum boat to have fun with her, but inside I was aching to just dive into the water and drown. In hindsight, I am sure she must have known my smiles were fake. But she was only eight years old, too young to understand what was going on—but old enough to suffer for it. I went to meetings almost daily. Sometimes I took Jenni with me, which wasn't a good idea. People in those meetings talk about things that children shouldn't have to hear, and I regret that I had to drag her to those places. Other times, I left her with Donna or with a babysitter. I was gone more now than I ever had been when I was drinking, and Jenni began to respond to this with her own anger. I found a therapy group for kids of alcoholics, which she participated in for a few months. I don't know if it helped her or not, but at least she was in a safe place to express her anger and with kids who were in the same boat. I know that I was not equipped to be an adequate mother for her. It was only after she was grown up that I learned parenting skills. If I was ever granted just one thing in life that I could do over, it would be the way I parented Jenni. I loved her more than life itself, and I wanted to be the best mother to her. I think she knew I loved her, but I wasn't a very good mom. I was angry a lot and I yelled all the time. I didn't even know I was yelling half the time. I had unrealistic expectations of her, and I didn't know when I should step in and run interference for her. I guess I expected her to be independent like I was. But it was an unfair expectation, and she struggled through her younger years. To this day, I have dreams about her as a young child, with me not able to properly care for her. I wake up with a weight of guilt that stays with me all day. It's something I don't know if I can ever forgive myself for.

As the depression bore down on me, I would spend my days keeping busy and holding my head up. At night, though, when Jenni was tucked into bed, I would begin to cry. I would be on the floor on all fours, pounding my fist on the floor, pulling my hair and sobbing so hard I couldn't breathe. I would collapse in a sweaty heap on the floor and sometimes fall asleep there, a sleep filled with horrible dreams. I felt so alone in the world. Yeah, I knew I had a higher power, but remember, my higher power was the river. It didn't come home with me. No one loved me. I was alone, scared, depressed, angry, and empty. I felt like an empty shell, and the pain of the emptiness was gut-wrenching.

When I was out in the world, I would see people walking down the street, talking, laughing, touching each other. Someone in their lives loved them. They were happy! Why couldn't I be happy at least once in a while? They weren't empty. I could see it in their eyes. There was something behind them. My eyes told me that there was nothing but pain and anger behind them. I just couldn't understand it. I wanted to die, but I couldn't kill myself now—I had a responsibility to be a mom, and I couldn't die like my mother did and leave Jenni without a mom. But was I good enough for her? I didn't think so. I felt that I didn't have anything to give her.

One evening in my therapy group, people were talking about love—people they loved and people who loved them. I started to fall apart. I didn't understand love. I knew I loved my daughter, and I thought she loved me. And I knew I had (or maybe still) loved Dick Forringer. But he didn't love me in return. And as far as I could tell, I loved my ex-husband, John, but he didn't love me, either. My father certainly didn't love me. And I doubted that my sister loved me. As I contemplated this, no longer listening to the group members, I felt like my insides were being wrenched apart. It occurred to me that besides my daughter, no one on this earth really loved me! No wonder I always felt so incredibly alone!

As people began to notice that big tears were running down my face, someone asked me, "Sara, what's wrong?"

After a long silence, without looking at anyone, I responded, "No one on earth loves me!" Another period of silence filled the room. I started to get on the floor, like I did at home when I felt like this, and then thought better of it. Barbara asked me what I was doing, and I said, "Well, at home, this is how I get through the night, after my daughter has gone to bed. I get on the floor and pound my fists. I try to pray, but I really don't know how to. I just feel so damned alone! I really have nothing to live for!"

Now I was afraid Barbara would send me to the state mental hospital, and they would throw away the key! They would dope me up with drugs, and there I would be until I died.

But Barbara didn't send me to the nuthouse. She did something even better. She loved me. She really did. I didn't understand it at first. Everyone kind of looked at their feet and then, out of the uncomfortable silence, Barbara said, "I love you." The room went silent. I stopped crying and said, "What?" She said, "I love you." She said it again and held my hand. I just looked at her and it slowly began to sink in.

"But how could you love someone as awful as me?"

"You're not awful—you are hurting. You have been injured, and you're fighting back. I love you with the love that God gives me—and it's unconditional. You are one of God's children, just like everyone in this room, worthy of love. You are lovable. I love you and God loves you, too."

I was thirty-three years old, and this was the first time anyone had ever said this to me, at least that I could remember. The exception, of course, was the men who were having sex with me and told me it was love. No one had ever told me they loved me before. I might have felt my mother's love when I was six years old, but that had been twenty-seven years ago. I had lived a lifetime since then, with no love. I had never loved myself. I had no concept of that. That was the message that caused me to stop drinking in the first place. Barbara's statement to me was so incredibly powerful. I really didn't understand the "love from God" part, but I believed her. The look in her eyes told me she was completely sincere. I felt something, just slightly, stir inside of me. When I left that night, I had a glimmer of hope.

CHAPTER 16

the pilot light

O ver the course of several weeks, I began to learn something extremely significant. *Learn* isn't the right word—it was more like *absorb*. When Barbara had said she loved me, and that I had been injured and was fighting back, I made an instant connection with the concept. My whole life had been a fight—a fight to live. Every step seemed like a battle, and every word I spoke was in defense of my life. I yelled at people all the time without even knowing I was yelling. Or maybe it was that I didn't know that other people didn't talk the way I did. What I slowly came to understand was that I was using my rage and anger to fight with—instead of my spirit. The men in my childhood had killed my spirit, or so I thought. All I had left were the injuries and rage and pain. Those things were the fuel that propelled me through life.

But the reality that I slowly came to believe was, they *didn't* kill my spirit. The piece that was missing was love. I needed love to reconnect with my inner spirit. After sitting by the river and taking long walks on the ocean's shore, I began to conceive the idea that my spirit was connected, through God, to all living creatures on earth. We're all connected. And we need each other, in spirit, to stay alive, to live, to carry on. We all have a spirit connection. We cannot live without it. Maybe this was what I was feeling when I watched the flow of the river. And maybe that was why I always loved going to the ocean.

I had been out of touch with my spirit for a long, long time—since I was a very little girl. This is why I had always felt so empty. The alcohol filled the emptiness and numbed the pain temporarily. But what was missing was my inner spirit that joined me with the rest of life on earth. I began to have a vision of it tucked away inside of me, like a pilot light, burning just enough to keep it going, like the pilot light in a stove. It was there the whole time, waiting for love to kindle a bigger flame.

Over the next couple of years, I began working rigorously on building up that flame. I wanted it to become a raging fire. I didn't want to be empty anymore. I needed to feel alive, to love and be loved and to be able to give love to my daughter—and receive love from her in return. I needed to join life instead of just fight for it.

It was suggested that I begin to pray, pray for anything—for acceptance, for willingness, for one day at a time—but just pray. This would be another big challenge for me, because how could I pray to a river? The people who told me to pray were talking about God, and I still didn't have that concept in my head yet. I thought God hated me because of the kind of person I had been most of my life. So I couldn't look Him in the eye, which is what I thought it meant to pray. It didn't make sense to pray to a river. So I began to do two things that worked for me. The first thing was to buy a journal with empty pages. I began to write down my prayers in it, letters to God. They went into the little book, and there I let them go. I wrote about my image of myself in the birdcage, and of dreams I was having about being in a boat that had no pilot and was running amok. I wrote about Barbara saying she loved me and how I made the connection with that to my spirit—my pilot light—and to the spirit of the rest of the world. I started writing in the prayer journal every night before going to bed. It seemed to work! If only slightly, I was beginning to feel a lift from my depression.

The other thing I did was go to Pemiquid Point, Maine—a place on the coast with an old lighthouse where the rocks jut out into the ocean. The surf there is wild most of the time, and I would go sit on the edge of the rocks to be near it. I felt that the closer to the edge I went, the closer to finding God I would get. I would sit on the rocks for long periods of time and just let the waves talk to me. I didn't hear voices—I simply let myself be open, and messages would come to me. I began keeping a little journal when I went there and I called it "Pemiquid Notes."

During those many days and nights in our little cabin following

my treatment, I had some time to just look at things through a
new set of eyes. One evening, while sitting in the dark (no longer
pounding the floor), I realized one thing that was missing in my life
was music. Oh, I had my stereo and records. But I didn't have my
piano anymore, and I couldn't make music. I knew I couldn't get a
piano into the little cabin, and I couldn't afford one. So I decided to
try to learn to play the guitar. The next day I went into a pawnshop
in Augusta and looked at all of the guitars they had for sale. I hadn't
a clue what to look for in a good guitar. But while I was in there,
two men came into the shop looking for guitars. One man picked
up each guitar, tuned it, and played a few chords. When he was
finished, he pointed to one of the guitars, and said, "This is the one
I want. I'm coming back to get it." When he left the shop, I picked
up that guitar and bought it for one hundred dollars. (I thought I was
pretty clever!)

I went home and began methodically teaching myself how to play
chords. It wasn't long before I was playing and singing some of
my old favorite songs. I would watch my daughter, Jenni, playing
with her things while I was strumming and singing, and it occurred
to me that once I got sober I had begun to see the world through
Jenni's eyes, and through her eyes I started my path to recovery. I
understood that the troubles she was having with school and friends
were my fault, and once I saw that, I moved on to seeing my situation
more clearly. A song began to form in my head as I strummed and
watched her quietly playing with her dolls. It came to symbolize my
awakening to a new life.

Jenni's Eyes

Today, I saw the morning sun come forth

Today, I heard the song of a bird

Today, I heard a baby cry

Oh God, I thank You for these things.

Today I awoke with a smile on my face
And looked into my Jenni's big brown eyes
And saw a life that I helped create
Oh God, I thank You for these things.

There were so many days I never saw the sun
I couldn't hear the birds singing their sweet songs
My Jenni's eyes were sad and filled with lonely pain
But God, You stood beside us all the way.

You brought me back so I could live again
You gave me a gift I never could give myself
The gift of life and living with Your love
Oh God, I thank You for my life.

Today is the first day of the rest of our lives
Today is an adventure through our love and faith
And with Your love my Jenni's eyes may never be sad again
Oh God, I thank You for my life.

Oh, and yes God, I thank You for Jenni's eyes.

It was nothing spectacular musically, but it was a testament to how important my recovery was and how important my daughter's life was, as well. She loved the song. I played my guitar and sang it a lot because it was like a prayer, and when I sang it I felt warm inside. It kept me keenly aware of how close I had come to losing everything.

I also decided that perhaps I could get to know who or what God was by going back to church. Since my adolescent experiences with church were with the Lutherans, I decided to attend the local Lutheran church. I got involved in the whole nine yards—choir, Sunday school, even the youth group. I took Jenni, but she never liked it. I went there for about five years, and aside from a nice relationship with a woman named Pat, I didn't get much out of it. I don't think it helped my concept of God at all. I never could buy the "original sin" argument, and I didn't think I could ever confide in anyone there about my life. I had told them I was a recovering alcoholic, and that was a huge mistake. Most people looked at me as though I were a leper. Although I tried to study the Christian Bible, I couldn't buy the virgin birth business, or accepting Jesus as my Savior (whatever that meant). I have no problem with people who do believe this, because it is a nice idea—especially the principles that Jesus purposed to have taught. At Christmas, I try to get in touch with a vision of peace, even if it is only in my own heart, and settle for that. But I didn't stay with the Lutheran church. I confess, I had been hoping it would be like the church I went to in Ashtabula. But that was a special place and it really couldn't be duplicated. It was what I needed at the time. (Those people were probably angels, too.)

Another suggestion that was given to me was that I get a sponsor. A sponsor is someone who is also a recovering alcoholic with some good, solid sobriety, preferably of the same gender, and someone who will make a commitment to help you get on with your sobriety. My first sponsor was a woman named Phyllis. She was about twenty years older than me and had three years of sobriety. To me, three years seemed like an eternity. She was very kind and patient with me. Her goal seemed to be to get me to turn my life over to a higher power. Wow! I sort of understood turning my disease over, but my whole life? Whew! I didn't know about that. Well, I had pretty much turned my life and will over to alcohol, right? As I listened to the principles of AA being recited at each meeting, I realized that they were saying "turn your life over." I really hadn't heard it like that before. Phyllis said it didn't matter what or who I thought God was. She didn't care if I turned it over to the river god of my understanding—she just wanted me to turn it over. But I had a difficult time with this concept. One day, she loaned me a little book that was all about—you guessed it—turning your life over to the God of your understanding. She said she wanted the book back in a week, because she needed it for someone else. There was only one line in the book that I remember to this day. It was significant in helping me to learn how to let go. My understanding of the book was that we must think of God as though He is a parent—like a mommy—and we are going to her with a cut finger, crying and asking her to kiss it and make it better. You know, when you go to your mommy, you know it's going to get better. It's kind of like the placebo effect—just knowing she is going to take care of it makes it feel better right away. I went back to my memories of my own mother, thinking about going to her with a cut finger. I was able to bring up a memory of how it felt to trust her to take care of me, and I realized I could try to do that with God. It was a breakthrough (it seemed like another miracle to me)! I called Phyllis and told her I had finished the book. She invited me to her house for dinner that evening and said I could bring the book back. I declined the invitation because I had no gas in my car—the gauge read *E*, and I had no money—not a cent. (I was still unemployed.) Phyllis said to me, "Why don't you trust God to take care of you?"

I said, "Well, He isn't going to put gas in my car—I can't just start driving with no gas and no way to get gas."

She kept insisting that I should just trust God and get in my car and come to see her. Finally, I got angry and said to myself, Alright, I'll show her. I'll drive my car and run out of gas and will have to walk home. That will fix her with her "trust in God" business! So I got in my car, with its empty gas gauge, and started driving. I stopped at the post office to get my mail and to my surprise, there was a letter from a friend—not from Phyllis—with a five-dollar bill in it and a note that said, "I know it's not much, but I hope it helps." (In 1981, five dollars was more than enough to put gas in your car!) I went to Phyllis's house and told her what happened, including the part about "I'll show her." Phyllis just smiled and gave me a hug. I can't tell you how many things like that happened to me over the years. It's just incredible! But I have Phyllis to thank for that. Unfortunately, Phyllis and her husband moved to California after about a year, and

I had to look for another sponsor.

My next sponsor was a man named Roland. Everyone called him Rolie. Although it was not advisable to get a sponsor that was of the opposite sex, Rolie was an exception to the rule. He was a sweet, kind man who wouldn't hurt a fly. He was actually as short as me, and had a hunchback from a childhood injury. His drinking had started in his early twenties because he felt like an outcast with his disfigured body. When I met him, he had twenty years of sobriety, was married to a woman named Lucille, and had three children. I knew I could trust him, and it was good for me to finally, for the first time in my life, have a healthy relationship with a man whom I could trust. He helped to restore my faith in men.

It was with Rolie that I did a lot of my soul-searching work with the twelve steps of AA. He knew that program inside and out. The twelve steps of AA are the backbone of the program. We spent a lot of evenings together in his house before meetings just talking, talking, talking. Rolie was wonderful for me and he helped me to move through those steps. The problem was that Rolie was sick. He had a lung disease that he was dying from. He had to start using oxygen twenty-four hours a day, carrying tanks on a little cart (which he referred to as "ET") everywhere he went. Eventually, he became homebound, so we started having meetings at his house. Those were special times. Rolie died in my second year of sobriety. His funeral was my first experience at a Catholic mass, and it was incredibly powerful. There were hundreds of AA people there, all of us crying and hugging. I missed him so much after that. At meetings, people would often refer to a joke he had told, or some wise statement he had made, and we would all realized that an angel had been in our midst. I will never forget the things I learned from him, nor will I ever forget the kind, gentle man he was.

An important process in the twelve-step recovery principles has to do with making amends to people you've hurt during your active phase of alcoholism. Rolie helped me with this. I began writing in a journal about people in my life who had been affected while I was actively drinking. My behavior was less than acceptable, and even though I couldn't explicitly remember many of the details, I knew many of the people whom I had hurt. One of them was my high school sweetheart, Dick Forringer. I had thought about him so many times over the years, and I always felt that our relationship was unresolved. He was married with two children now, and lived in North Carolina. He probably had forgotten who I was! But I felt I needed to apologize for how I had behaved those last weeks we were going together. And I felt I should tell him what was going on in my house when we were dating. Perhaps this would help him to understand my strange behavior. But, moreover, this would be the soul work I needed to do to get on with my own recovery. I needed to be able to forgive myself. So I sat down and wrote a short, to-the-point letter explaining my newfound sobriety and a brief explanation about the incest that happened with my father so many years ago. I also apologized for going out with his friend (some "friend," huh?) and for my unrealistic expectations of him. It was scary to write this letter, but once I made the commitment to do it, the words just flowed onto the paper. The moment I dropped it into the mailbox, I felt a sense of relief. I realized that this business of making amends had incredible value to my peace of mind. I didn't expect an answer from him and I even thought that I might get the letter back undeliverable. So imagine my surprise when I received a letter from him after only one week! It was a long letter, saying,

> I so much appreciated hearing from you! I thought about you as well over the years. I knew something awful was going on in your house back when we were dating, but I didn't know what it was. I always knew your father physically abused you girls, but I didn't think there was anything anyone could do about it.

He said he was married and had two boys (one the same age as Jenni) and that he was teaching math at a private school in Durham, North Carolina. They sounded so happy. I realized he could have never been that happy if he had married me. I smiled as I tucked the letter away for safe keeping, and felt a little glow inside me that seemed to stay with me. I crossed his name off of my huge amends list. I began writing other letters to people out in California. Some of them wrote back and didn't seem to understand why I was writing;

they thought I had slipped a gear. I didn't care. I knew that quite the opposite was happening—that the gears in my brain were finally working right! Other letters came back with "address unknown" stamped on the envelope. I saved them, though I'm not sure why. I knew the commitment and effort of making amends had been made, and that was what I needed to do.

After three months of unemployment, and eating wormy fish out of the lake every day, I finally found a job. It wasn't a great job, but it was still a job—as a legal secretary for a large firm of lawyers. They didn't pay well, and they had very little sympathy for the fact that I was a single mom and a recovering alcoholic. But it was a job. On wintry mornings, they wouldn't allow me to go to work a few minutes late so that I could see Jenni off on the school bus. I had to drive to work, leaving her standing alone on the edge of the road waiting for the bus. Many days, I just couldn't do it, and I would pay dearly when I got to work late. I was lucky they didn't fire me.

The most difficult part of that job came when I began to unravel some of the most painful memories of my childhood. I had completed my work in the women's therapy group and entered another therapy group for incest survivors. The work we did there, such as writing no-mail letters to our perpetrators and to other family members, served to bring more detailed memories to the surface. It was incredibly painful work, and I lost a lot of sleep. I was afraid to go to sleep at night because the nightmares became stranger than ever. I no longer had my friend, alcohol, to numb the pain. And in my new job, I had to type depositions by men who had been charged with crimes of sexual assault against their children. These were detailed accounts of what they did, and their narcissistic twist on the behavior. It was excruciating to have to work on these cases, but the lawyer I worked for, who was defending these men, wouldn't give the cases to another secretary, saying it would not be fair. He said he had empathy for my situation, but I don't think he really cared. I was working on a plan to get another job. In the meantime, I started the first noontime AA meeting in Augusta, so that I would have a safe place to escape to during the day while I was working. I think that meeting is still running to this day.

When I was sober just a year, I received a phone call from Dick Forringer. You could have blown me over with a feather! I would have known his voice anywhere, even though it had been at least fifteen years since I had talked to him. He said that shortly after his letter to me, he and his wife separated. His wife had been cheating on him, not for the first time, and he just couldn't take it anymore. He wanted to come to Maine and visit me. He came a few weeks later and stayed four days. When I met him at the airport, we flew into each other's arms and he picked me up and twirled me around, just like Tracy and Hepburn in the movies! We had a whirlwind four days, with very little sleep and lots of talking and walking in the woods. I even took him to an AA meeting with me. It was a good visit, and when he left, we agreed it wouldn't be the last. We had several visits, with and without our children, back and forth between Maine and North Carolina over several years. The relationship never developed to the commitment stage, and it took me a long time to realize that it never would. I eventually came to realize that the "love" I felt for him was out of proportion. I had seen him in my teen years as a savior from my father and the life I was stuck in. The feelings I had for him were very real, but not realistic. He was just a guy, not a saint. When I stood back and took a good, objective look at the situation, I realized, painfully, that we really had nothing in common, and neither one of us wanted to move away from where we were living. We did have a lot of fun together, though, and I will always have a special place in my heart for him and cherish his presence in my life. He seems more like family to me, since I knew him before my mother died. He is one of the few people on earth who can remember my mother. We still stay in touch via e-mail.

Jenni and I quickly outgrew our little cabin on the lake, and I longed to be in my own home. After an exhausting search, with a very patient real estate agent, I found a little house on the outskirts of Augusta that was just perfect for us, and we moved in at the end of October 1983. The house had been lived in previously by a man who was a violent alcoholic; he had punched holes in the walls and torn doors off their hinges. The house and I would recover together. I also made the commitment that there would be no cigarette smoking in this house, and I quit when I moved in. I found that quitting smoking was harder than quitting alcohol had been. I got a little crazy and gained weight from substituting smoking with eating. But I used the same principles I had used earlier in my recovery from alcoholism and they worked for me. I have never had another cigarette since then! And, I'm healthier for it.

After reading an article in a magazine about a group of women in California who started a twelve-step support group for survivors of incest, I wrote to them and received information and materials on starting my own group. I wrote letters to a dozen or so churches in the area until I received an answer from one. I went to meet the minister, a wonderful man named David Glusker. Although I didn't know it at the time, he was a bit of a celebrity in Maine, with his own morning devotion television program. He was a kind, gentle man who offered to let me hold my group meetings in his church, free of charge. He even offered his time for counseling, supervision, or whatever I needed to be able to run this group. I think he knew more than I did that it would take a lot out of me, and be quite stressful. I started the group with a handful of people whom I had met in AA and my therapy group. I wanted to share the leadership with other women, but there was never anyone who could take it over. It became evident, though, that this type of support group was incredibly helpful for sexual abuse survivors. We felt a special bond with each other, and gradually felt safe in talking about our experiences. I suggested we write "no-mail" letters to not only our perpetrators, but to others in our family, like our mothers, who stood by and let this happen to us. We wrote the letters, and then took turns reading them out loud. It was quite therapeutic. Then I suggested we have a bonfire and ceremoniously toss the letters into the fire, with a farewell to our "victim" selves. With that, we became survivors! Very soon, I began receiving phone calls from both the psychiatric unit at the Augusta General Hospital and the Augusta Mental Health Institute, asking if they could send their patients to my group. I was a little hesitant, concerned that it might not be safe for them to come out into the community. The first person who came was accompanied by a counselor who didn't attend the group, but sat outside and waited. Once it was established that this woman would be able to attend these meetings safely, she could then come alone. The catch was, I was to pick her up and return her back to the State hospital. She was a very troubled woman, and she might never be able to live out on her own. I'm not sure that these group meetings did her any good. But it helped me to have her there. I'll never forget one night when I was taking her back to the unit, with the sound of the steel doors locking behind me as I left alone, I realized that, but for a few angels and a couple of miracles, I could have been in that place, too. Most of the people there had come from childhoods like mine. How did I escape this? I was overwhelmed with gratitude, to the point of tears. As I was driving away, I stopped my car on the street, got out, and walked down the sidewalk. Two people approached me, and I only stepped aside, but I stayed on the sidewalk! It was an incredible breakthrough. I felt worthy of occupying my half of the sidewalk! And they didn't stop me! It was a wonderful experience, and I have that poor woman to thank. (Another angel.)

Another incredible experience happened because of that group. One night, a woman left her family and headed toward the Kennebec River with plans to jump off the bridge and kill herself. On her way down the street, she looked up at the church and saw a lone light burning in an upstairs room. She felt so drawn to that room that she went up. There we were, almost waiting for her to come in! She asked why we were meeting, and I told her. She sat down, buried her head in her knees, and sobbed. She had been plagued her whole life because of sexual abuse in her childhood. Now she was concerned that her husband was abusing her own children, and she felt completely powerless. She was scared and not thinking clearly. Believing it was the only way out of the pain, she planned to kill herself. Instead, she joined our group. It was incredible! She eventually left her husband, realized her lifelong dream, and became the first female firefighter in the Augusta Fire Department!

The group lasted about two years. I ended it only because it wore me out. I could never find anyone who could or would share the leadership with me. And I just didn't have the energy to do it alone anymore. But I do believe the group was very good for my recovery process, as well as for many other women.

During my second year of sobriety, I was invited to do some

volunteer work running aftercare groups at Seton Hospital. I was thrilled to have the opportunity to do this—to give back some of which had been given to me. I had also started taking courses at the University of Maine. I was pleasantly surprised that they gave me credit for all of the courses I had taken at Kent State back in 1966–67. I earned an associate's degree in social services. I was very fortunate to get a job at New Directions as a substance abuse counselor, even before I finished my coursework. One problem, which I didn't see at the time, was that I went to work at same place I had done my own therapy. Barbara, the facilitator of my group, was now my clinical supervisor. This would prove to be a huge challenge for my sobriety, as well as an opportunity to keep growing emotionally and spiritually.

I began to have many tearful meetings with Barbara, and I couldn't understand why I was so miserable. I had no idea that going to work in the place where I had done all of this recovery work, dumped all of my secrets for safekeeping, would be so difficult for me. In hindsight, it was the worst thing anyone can do, at least that early in the recovery process. Really, they should have never hired me. I wouldn't advise this to anyone. It was as though I had gone back to wallow around in my own shit! No, it was as though I had moved back home with my alcoholic family! It was horrible. I kept asking Barbara for help, and her response was, "This is your problem. You need to figure out what to do. I can't help you." I was brokenhearted. I had thought she loved me! Well, I eventually realized that I was wallowing in self-pity. And I also realized that I had put her on a pedestal with unfair expectations. Subconsciously, I think I made her into my *mother*.

It was suggested to me that I needed to go do some grief work regarding my mother's death. This didn't make sense to me—she had died so long ago. Surely, I had already done my grieving. But, I soon realized that I hadn't done any at all. No one in my childhood years would let me do it—they didn't know how themselves! I had been hanging on to a fantasy about my mother as an angel, sitting on my shoulder all of my life, and I needed to move on and let her go.

I started seeing a therapist, Chris York, who specialized in grief work. He got right to the heart of things. He asked me to bring in a picture of her so I could talk to her in my sessions. I dug out her high school senior picture and put it in a frame. Back in the 1940s, portraits were made to look like paintings, by painting over a black-and-white photo with color, to make the lips red and put color in the hair. But the effect was a picture that looked like a black-and-white photo that had been painted over. The skin was ashen and the lips were too red. But I never noticed that. She was my mother—she was beautiful and the quality of the picture was something I had never considered. When I began to "talk" to my mother's picture as Chris suggested, I had no idea where he was going with this. He said to me, "Sara, she's dead. Look at the picture—it looks like a corpse. Her skin is even white! She's not really in the room." Oh my God, I couldn't believe he was saying this! But, painfully, I realized he was right. I began crying and sobbing, and over many tearful sessions, I finally said good-bye to her—but only after letting her know that I was angry at her for giving me such a difficult chore when she died, to take care of my father and sisters, and then leaving me with those lecherous men in my family who would maul over me all those years. It was a new concept to let myself be mad at her. How do you get mad at someone who is dead? But that was what I needed to do. Eventually, though, I forgave her and said good-bye. I knew I would see her again someday—a long time from now.

This was hard and painful work, but necessary. It left me feeling a little more empty, though. I felt like a little girl, standing alone, with no one to take my hand. I started having flashbacks of my childhood, and my dreams became very frightening. The incest by my father and sexual abuse by my uncles and grandfather were still there, and I felt like I was reliving it over and over on a daily basis, with nothing to numb the pain or shield me from the fear. Although I didn't understand what was happening, I began having periods of dissociation. That is, I would be talking with someone and it would suddenly feel like I was going backward down a long tunnel, and the person I was talking with was getting farther and farther away. Their voice would seem to almost disappear, and I would not even know what they were saying. Almost anything would trigger this, and I never knew what would cause it. People would touch my shoulder and say things like "Are you okay? Are you feeling alright? Are you still there?" And I wouldn't even know why they were saying this. I would come out of my trancelike state and stumble through some explanation of why I hadn't been paying attention. I began to realize that this was what I had done when I was in school and would miss entire classes or not know what a teacher was talking about when he called on me—back when they called me "Sahara Dry Run"! What I didn't realize was that dissociation was a safety net that my body-mind system used to protect me from the pain of the memories. I hadn't known it had a name or that it happened to other people. I had just thought again and again that I was going crazy.

Despite my progress, anger and rage continued to be a common thread in my life. I could fake it sometimes and smile and be nice and polite. But it would only take a word or a facial expression to turn me into a raging, angry woman. I began to see this theme repeating itself and wondered why my recovery wasn't growing, why I wasn't growing spiritually, why the anger and rage were still there. It wore me out, it wore out my friends, and it especially wore out my sister. I yelled at people with no provocation and I rarely smiled. I began to see that the anger and rage was a toxic energy force within me and was tethering me to one spot, preventing emotional and spiritual growth. I also knew that the anger came directly from my childhood experiences, mostly with my father. I decided I had to find a way to let go of it. I had this image of pulling a trailer filled with hate and anger and rage behind me. It was just boiling over but I was stuck with it tied to me. I could ignore it, but every time I turned around, it was still there, seething away, ready to ruin another friendship. How do you let go of something like that? I began to pray about it, asking for guidance.

The answer that came up for me was that I had to *forgive*. Oh my God! How would I ever do that? I started talking to people who had done some of this work, who had forgiven unforgivable acts. How did they do it? Did it mean that I had to say what was done to me was actually okay? I knew I couldn't do that. No, it didn't mean that. It meant that I had to let go of the anger, give it back to the person or persons who gave it to me, by forgiving. I had to leave the trailer alongside the road, to never carry it with me again. So I kept this image of the trailer full of boiling, bubbling anger and rage, and one night, while alone at home, I lit a candle, sat on the floor in the middle of the room, held out my hands, and said out loud, "I let go of it. I don't want it anymore. It is killing me. I want to live. Please take it away from me." Tearfully, I gave it up. I mentally untied the imaginary trailer full of hate and left it behind. It was an incredibly powerful few moments that would change the path of my life for the better. It was as though a huge weight was lifted from my shoulders, and I felt the toxic anger begin to seep out of me. It was not all gone, though, and it would take a long time and more work for me to get rid of it all.

But something miraculous happened only a few days after this. I received a phone call from my father! I hadn't talked to him in a long time, and I didn't want to. And he didn't know about the work I was doing on my childhood issues. I wondered if he even remembered them. So when he called me, I should have been scared—my heart should have started pumping fast and I should have started shaking. That had always been my reaction until now whenever I talked to him. But this time was different. And when he started talking, I realized that a miracle was happening. He said to me through tears and sniffles, "Sara, I don't know what to do. I can't walk down the street and hold my head up anymore. I can't look in the mirror. I can't do anything."

I knew what he was talking about, but I needed to hear it from him. So I said, "What are you talking about, why can't you hold your head up?"

His answer was "Because of what I did to you when you were a girl. No father should ever do those things. I can't live with myself anymore. I don't know how you have managed all these years. I know you're struggling, Donna has said so. I know it was what ruined your marriage. And I know it's because of me. I just don't know what to do about it."

There was a period of silence, and then I said to him, "Dad, I have forgiven you." More silence. I said again, "Dad, I have forgiven you."

Finally, through his tears, he said, "How can you do that?"

I said, "I'm not really sure, but I'm not doing this alone. I am in counseling and I pray about this all the time. I am forgiving you. I'm not saying what happened was okay, I'm saying I can't be angry about it anymore, and I can't blame you for my unhappiness anymore. I go to AA and I'm staying sober, and I have to do this for my own peace of mind and my own continued mental health. What you should do is go get counseling so you can hold your head up again. I am letting you go. You're free to go take care of yourself, and know that I am taking care of myself."

It was a powerful phone call, one that left me feeling like that pilot light was beginning to build a bigger fire and my one unit of worth was growing. The emptiness was beginning to be replaced with something good. It was exhausting work. Whenever anything like this would happen, I would just sleep for days from exhaustion. Then I would get up and feel like starting a new day, a new life, a new beginning, all over again.

It was through my counseling job at New Directions that I met Jeremy. I had to go to court to testify on a case involving a client who was on probation, and Jeremy was the assistant district attorney who was prosecuting the case. He sat with me for about a half hour prior to the hearing to let me know what kind of questions he would be asking me on the stand. He wanted to know my answers. He seemed a little more personal than I would have expected. I guess I'm just naïve about such things, because I later realized he was flirting with me. He seemed like a nice guy. A few weeks later, when the case was all finished, he called me and invited me out to lunch. He turned out to be a nice man, with a lot more class than anyone I had been out with before. We ended up dating for almost a year, and then I invited him to move in with me. One day, while the two of us were in our bedroom, he was starting to undress to go to bed. He pulled his belt out off in one big swoop, and I noticed something happening to me. I experienced a surge of emotions, one right after the other in a span of a few seconds. First it was fear—stark terror—then rage, and then an angry voice came from my mouth with words I could not comprehend. Jeremy looked at me and asked me what the heck I was talking about, touching me on the shoulder. When he touched me, I realized I was in that dissociative state again, but because I felt somewhat safe, I was in a space to be able to sort it out. I recognized the trigger was the belt—he pulled it off the same way my father used to, sometimes for a beating and sometimes when he was undressing to climb into bed with me. I talked about it with Jeremy, and it seemed to put me into a different place of understanding. I realized that there were probably other simple triggers in everyday life that would send me into this state at any place or time. I decided to pay more attention to this so I could control it better. I was still having problems with unwarranted angry outbursts and had been told more than once by people that I was too loud, too rude, too confrontational, and a lot of people just didn't like me. I thought that forgiving would just take care of it all, but it didn't. But I think some of this stuff—the memories—are embedded in your body. The body parts carry the memory, and they wait to be triggered and fester up. Even though I had let go of the trailer full of anger, my brain cells and the memories on my insides were still there. It was a physiological reality. The dissociation and angry outbursts were not something I had control of—until now. Now I had an explanation. It was a painful piece of insight to realize how people had seen me—very different from the way I wanted to see myself. I still had a lot of work to do.

Although I believed I loved Jeremy, and it was good to have him there, an ugly truth began to emerge. He couldn't keep his secret from me—the fact that he used drugs. I had begun to notice strange behavior. He would air out the car when he came home from anywhere, for no apparent reason. (He was letting the smell of marijuana escape.) Sometimes he would be sitting at the table eating, and his head would just drop and he would almost pass out. I thought it was narcolepsy, but then there were other things. Jenni said he had driven erratically with her on several occasions, and when she told me this, I wouldn't let her ride with him anymore. Then one day, while looking in his desk for something, I found a razor blade and a small mirror, with white powder residue on it. That's what cocaine addicts use to take a hit. When I figured it out, I was furious—and scared. What had I done? How on earth did I let that slip by me? And what was an assistant district attorney doing prosecuting people for using drugs when he himself was doing the same thing? Now the question for me was, what to do about it? I went to Al-Anon and asked for help, then made a plan to confront him with it. One night when he came home late (I later learned that he had been at his drug dealer's house), I met him in the driveway and confronted him with my suspicion about his drug use. He, of course, denied the whole thing. I even offered to help him get into treatment, telling him I'd support him through the whole process if he would just ask for help, but he continued to deny his drug use. So I gave him five minutes to gather a change of clothes, then asked—told—him to leave and not come back. It was very scary. I don't actually know what I was scared of. He wasn't aggressive or mean or violent in any way. I was just scared of having a drug user in my house, not only because of my own sobriety and my job, but because of Jenni, who was now twelve years old and very impressionable. Not to mention that he was driving her places in his car, under the influence! So he left, and I was brokenhearted. I really grieved this loss. I felt like someone had kicked me in the stomach. But I still had my pilot light to guide me and to keep me safe. It gave me the energy to keep going. I knew, painful as it was, that I had done the right thing. I had learned about the grieving process earlier in my recovery. Now I had a chance to do it again. Lucky me.

I was still having trouble making friends. Barbara seemed to truly have unconditional love—something I had never experienced. I also had met another friend early in my recovery, Betty F. I liked her because she had an inner spiritual quality I really hadn't seen in most people I met in recovery (besides Barbara). She was easy to talk to and we had children the same age. Her son Tony was her youngest of five. She was a nurse and was going through a divorce. We both embraced the twelve steps in much the same way. She also didn't seem to judge me harshly because of my aggressiveness. I appreciated that in her. But most people thought I was loud and rude and in too much of a hurry. I did everything at top speed. I skipped steps when climbing stairs; I ran when walking would be more sensible. I talked fast and washed the dishes fast and drove fast. I started putting the slogan "Easy does it" all over everything, my steering wheel, the phone, the door to my house so I would see it when going out. But my energy was still, in part, fueled by the rage that continued to boil inside of me. Although I was doing a lot of work on my childhood trauma issues, I still hated my father and uncles, and the hate became a toxic energy inside of me, interfering with my recovery. At some point, I realized that I would have to find a way to let go of that bitterness, but I wasn't sure how to do it.

Late at night, in our little house, I would write in my journal and play my guitar and sing. These simple pleasures brought me some peace, and helped me to see my path a little clearer. Quite by accident, I found a poster with a picture of a bouquet of flowers on it. At the bottom it said: *"Happiness is the art of making a bouquet of those flowers within reach."* It was a revelation to me. It meant that I should stop looking outside me for happiness, but rather look inside—into my own soul—to find happiness. This was a new concept. So one night, I sat down and wrote a little story. You might say it was a children's story. But to me it was a lesson learned with much pain. The story goes like this:

The Little Frog and the Lily Pad

Once upon a time, there was a little frog who was very unhappy. He decided to leave the swamp he lived in and go out into the world and seek happiness. He started hopping from lily pad to lily pad. Each time he hopped, he would slip off the lily pad. Instead of climbing back onto it to rest for a while, he just hopped to another one, never stopping to look around him.

For years and years the little frog hopped all over lily pads in many different swamps. After a while, he became haggard-looking and very thin. He never even allowed himself time to eat or sleep properly. One day, he came upon a big, fat frog surrounded by several little tadpoles, all sitting on a big overgrown lily pad. This big frog looked so happy! The little frog decided to stop and ask the big frog how he got so happy, and how he had found such a big lily pad.

"Big Frog," he asked between gasps of breath, "how did you get so fat, and why are you so happy, and where on earth did you get that huge lily pad?"

"Whoa!" said the big frog. "One question at a time. Why don't you sit down and have some bugs with us and rest awhile, and I will tell you my story."

"Oh, I haven't got time! I have to run out and find my happiness! Please make your story short." said the little frog.

"Well," started the big frog, "perhaps that is just where I will start my story. I never do anything in a hurry. If I did, I would miss too much. So if you would please take the time to eat some bugs with us and rest awhile, I can answer your questions."

The little frog thought about it for a minute or two and then moaned, "Oh, alright, I guess I can stay awhile." He picked up a big juicy bug, bigger and juicer than any he had ever seen!

The big frog made himself comfortable, lit his pipe, and began to tell his story. "I must tell you," he began, "I didn't find happiness—it found me."

"But how on earth did happiness ever find you?" interrupted the little frog, with his mouth full of juicy bugs.

The big frog began, "I came to this lily pad a long time ago. It wasn't as big as it is now, but I wasn't so big either." He patted his stomach. "It looked like a good enough lily pad, so I stayed. I just decided to make the best with what I had and to enjoy what was around me. The lily pad grew over the years, and so did I. One day, quite some time ago, I met a lovely young lady frog. She liked my lily pad, so we became friends. The next thing you know, we were married and had a lot of little tadpoles."

"But where is your wife now?" asked the little frog.

With a tear in his eye, the big frog answered, "I'm sorry to say, she died awhile back. I will stay here, though, and raise my children until they are big. I have a lot of friends who help me, since I am getting old now."

The little frog interrupted again, "I had a friend once, but she had a funny lump on her head, and she didn't like the color of my eyes, so she wasn't really a friend."

The big frog puffed on his pipe and said, "Sounds like you didn't really give the friendship a chance."

"Oh shucks!" said the little frog. "Nobody will ever want to be my friend. Look at me! I'm skinny and tired and all worn out. And I don't have a lily pad of my own. I guess your kind of happiness just isn't for me. I just don't understand."

With that, the little frog started rubbing his eyes and began to cry. He was so very tired and lonely. "Anyway, I can't really do anything for anyone. I've never met anyone who doesn't have something special that he can do. I can't do anything. I guess I'll just have to go on being lonely and unhappy. Guess happiness isn't for everyone."

The little frog was preparing to start hopping off the lily pad and be on his way when the big frog said, "Where are you going? You're too sick and thin to go on like that. Why don't you stay here for a while? We have plenty of room."

The little frog scratched his head and said, "I don't understand. Why would you want me around? I wouldn't want someone like me around."

The big frog put his big hand on the little frog's shoulder and said, "Please sit down, son." So the little frog, being really tired, sat down one more time. The big frog spoke very softly but firmly. "You're so thin because you've been running and running and hopping and hopping all of your life. You're unhappy because you have never stopped long enough to see if you liked anything around you. You're lonely because you don't have any friends. You see, I learned a long time ago, in order to make friends, you first have to be a friend. And to have someone else like you, you must first like yourself. You can't find happiness by running to it. You must make do with what you have and enjoy what you have around you. When you can achieve that, happiness will come to you—from inside of you. Then, if you choose to move to another lily pad or another swamp, you can take your happiness with you. You don't' have to live your life like I do. Not everyone needs to get married. It takes different things to make different frogs happy."

The big frog was quiet for a few moments and took time to relight his pipe then stand and stretch and catch a few bugs. Then he asked the little frog, "Would you like to stay here with us for a while until you can get healthy?"

"But what can I do? I'd just be in the way. I can't pay you rent or anything."

The big frog answered, "You can do something very useful for me if you want to."

"What on earth can I do for you?" asked the little frog, really confused now. "You're a very good hopper."

"My little tadpoles are soon going to be frogs and will need to be taught how to hop. I'm so old, I can't teach them. Arthritis, you know. You could stay and teach them how to hop, and that would pay your rent. You might even make some friends. And there are plenty of bugs here for everyone. Would you like to do that?"

Well, the little frog had never been offered anything so wonderful in his life. He had to think about this. He even waited till the next day to make up his mind (which is the slowest he had ever done anything in his whole life).

When the big frog got up the next morning, he saw that the little frog had all the tadpoles (who were now turning into frogs) lined up on the lily pad. He was teaching them to hop. He noticed that the little frog had a smile on his face, and he lit his pipe and sat down, giving a wink to the little frog as he passed by.

We will never really know if the little frog found his happiness. But it is a sure bet that this was the happiest day of his life.

The End

Writing that story was an exercise in learning something I should have learned in my childhood. No one was there to teach it to me. I started, if only slightly, to slow down a bit, to look around and smell the roses.

I eventually quit my job at New Directions and went to work in a detoxification unit at a hospital in Waterville as a substance abuse counselor. I started learning that people who work for these programs aren't always recovering alcoholics, and some of the people haven't done their own work. Working in these environments could be compared to being in an alcoholic family with most of the same dynamics present. Why had I done this to myself—put myself right back into my family? The problem was that I was using my own experiences to help other people, so I had to relive my pain each time I went into a counseling session with a patient. But at this point, I didn't know what else to do for a living, and it only seemed to make sense to help other alcoholics get sober. I decided to take some more classes on psychology and counseling, and I eventually realized that I didn't need to work from my gut all the time, that I could use the skills I had been learning to help people and not have to draw from my own pain each time. It took a lot of work and practice to develop this skill, however.

Now that I was no longer working at New Directions and Barbara was no longer my clinical supervisor, I started to learn more about her and our friendship began to grow. We would go out to dinner together, and sometimes to meetings together. We did regular things together that I had never really learned to do in sobriety. She was in recovery, too—about twenty years longer than me. She was a terrific role model for me, and a wonderful person to have as a friend. Our friendship has grown over the years. I love her dearly and there isn't a thing on this earth I wouldn't do for her.

After Jeremy left, I tried dating another man, someone I had met through my sister. In hindsight, it wasn't wise to jump into another relationship so soon, but I was still down the road from learning this. Although Bob didn't drink or use drugs, he was emotionally immature and had a lot of issues he had never addressed from his own childhood. The result was a very troubled man with poor communication skills, with no connection to his emotions, and with sexual impotence. In a way, the last part was a relief because I still didn't like having sex with a man. I began to hide a little secret that had been creeping into my brain for a long time. I kept thinking about being with a woman. I had a couple of friends who were lesbians, and I desperately wanted to find out more about their lifestyle. Sometimes I would ask indirect questions, but I didn't really get the answers I wanted. I needed to be more direct, but I was afraid to do so. My daughter was an adolescent, and I felt that it could very well ruin her teen years and my relationship with her if I "came out" as a lesbian. Kids have a tough enough time finding a way to fit into the world without having to be told their mother is all of a sudden a queer! So, despite the tugging and nagging going on inside me, I kept quiet about it for a long time. In fact, I decided I just wouldn't act on it, because I wasn't sure I could live with the resulting problems that would arise.

Eventually, I had the opportunity to go to work for the State of Maine in the licensing department for the Office of Substance Abuse. I began working as a licensing and monitoring specialist, which meant I went to all of the treatment centers around the state inspecting them for their license renewal, and opening new programs. I really loved this job. It felt like a step up from being a counselor. And I didn't have to go through the pain of hearing people's stories all day. On a licensing visit to the hospital in Bangor, I found myself face-to-face with Dr. Evans, the man who had helped guide me into my new life of sobriety. Now, it was me with the big stick! I had mixed feelings about him. He was such a knowledgeable doctor in the field of chemical dependency, but he had such a horrible bedside manner. I had deep admiration for him, and at the same time I was angry at him for the emotional abuse he put me through while I was in treatment. However, he was considered the guru on addictions in the state of Maine, and I really wanted to learn from him. Working with him at this level was a good experience for me. It gave me another notch toward my unit of self-worth that Barbara had granted me, but that I was still building. I realized that I was now in a position of respect and trust on a subject that was almost the cause of my death. It was awesome!

At the same time, my youngest sister, Joyce, was still living in California. She was still on drugs—heroin—and she had gotten married to another heroin addict. They had a baby, and miraculously, the child was born okay. But for some reason, she named her after my daughter, even with the same middle name! I really didn't understand this. But what can you do? When her daughter was four years old, her husband discovered he had liver cancer. He died after a long, painful time of suffering. I learned that Joyce had been stealing his pain medication and filling his IV with just plain water. I remember once talking with her on the phone, hearing him screaming in pain in the background, not knowing that Joyce had taken his pain meds. After he died, Joyce's drug addiction got worse, and her daughter, at age five, called 911 after finding Joyce on the floor with a needle in her arm and unresponsive. She saved her mother's life. I don't understand why no one took the child away from her. But then, shortly after that, she announced that she was "clean" and was going to NA and AA and was in counseling! This was a real breakthrough. Joyce had been into drugs and alcohol since she was thirteen years old, and she had never gotten into recovery. If she was truly in recovery now, this was a miracle. Then she decided to come to Maine! I wasn't excited about this—I didn't want her here. She would be nothing but trouble. I was finally getting my life in order, and I didn't need her to get in the way. I was quite selfish, I will admit. She wanted me to go to California and drive the U-Haul truck with her and Jenny and her dog back to Maine. I refused to do it. I knew it would be crazy-making and I didn't think I could stand to be trapped in a vehicle that long with her. So, after shaming me for not going to help her, Donna went. From what I've heard through Donna, the experiences of that trip could be the subject of another whole book!

Shortly after Joyce moved to Maine, she started having serious emotional problems. She was depressed, crying all the time, and couldn't seem to manage day-to-day life—she was even more dysfunctional than me. She had a livable income from Social Security from the death of her husband, and she could actually get by without working. But she still couldn't manage. If she was truly in recovery from her addictions, she had not really done much work around the stuff from our childhood. In hindsight, I think she had a lot of issues that were probably impossible to resolve because of how young she was when our mother died. When children experience trauma at a "pre-verbal" age, it becomes very difficult for them to talk about it in adulthood. Because it happened before they were talking, they don't have words to remember it and can't even talk about it or frame a story about it. Even if memories come up, they only come up as fragmented flashbacks that make no sense, and they cause torment and emotional pain. Joyce just wasn't equipped to deal with these issues. But, at the time, I didn't understand all that. Joyce was suffering in a painful vacuum, much worse than I was, but she was ill equipped to address it.

I had recently been asked to become a member of the board of directors for a women's substance abuse treatment center called Crossroads for Women. They had a residential program out in the country treating addictions and also a relapse prevention track for two weeks. I thought this might be something Joyce could go to, so I gave her one of the brochures to look at. A few days later, she told me she had called them and had an appointment for a screening. She asked if I would take her, and I said I would. She went to the two-week relapse prevention program there, and came home with a new attitude. She began taking antidepressant medication and was going to therapy. For the first time in our lives together, I could have a realistic conversation with her. But after six months or so, she decided that since she was feeling so good, she would stop taking the medication and she quit going to counseling. She went back to her old self again, and I believe she relapsed. She never said so, but as I look back, I believe that is what was going on. She was difficult to be around, she was argumentative, and every conversation left me a little confused about what had transpired. I felt sorry for her daughter, Jenny, because Joyce tried to live her life vicariously through Jenny's. Jenny was in gymnastics and Joyce pushed her very hard to keep doing better, winning more meets and getting more ribbons and medals. I think Joyce thought Jenny could go to the Olympics. I'm not sure that's what Jenny wanted. Joyce had such a hard time with life, I can't even imagine what it was like to live with her as a mother.

It was while working for the state that I reconnected with Jeremy.

On a licensing visit to an agency on the coast, I ran into a man named Bob who looked vaguely familiar to me. He told me that he knew me through Jeremy, which threw me for a loop, because I hadn't connected him with Jeremy. At any rate, he said he and Jeremy were good friends and that Jeremy was now enjoying his third year of sobriety! I was thrilled to learn this, and hoped that perhaps my intervention had done some good after all! Sometime during the following week, I actually ran into Jeremy at my bank, where, coincidentally, he did his banking. We exchanged greetings and brief updates about our kids and went on our merry way. Then— what are the chances of this? I ran into him again at the supermarket! This time, he was even more friendly—actually flirting with me. He asked me to go out to dinner with him sometime, because he felt he must make amends to me, as he was really "working his program." I agreed to meet him for dinner. This seemed like a good thing.

The dinner was at a restaurant near the Augusta Airport, and next to the Maine Instrument Flight School. I had driven past that place a hundred times, each time saying to myself, Someday I will stop in there and see about learning to fly. Jeremy was gracious and kind, more so than I had ever remembered him to be. He seemed to truly be in sobriety, and he actually thanked me for my intervention on him. He said he knew he was out of control, and when I confronted him, he moved into an apartment in Portland and got stoned every day for two months, then went and asked for help. He was now about three years sober and genuinely apologized to me for the hurt he had caused me. I accepted his apology and decided this was another step in my search for my whole unit of worth. I had done something good for someone. Then he began talking about the fact that he was taking flying lessons, and wondered if I had ever tried it. I felt my heart do an about-face! No, I told him, I hadn't done that yet. But I would someday. It was just that someday hadn't arrived yet. He offered to give me a gift of an introductory flight lesson, and I quickly said yes before he could change his mind! This also meant that I might see him again, a thought that didn't altogether seem like a bad idea.

CHAPTER 17

the pilot

The introductory flight happened a couple of weeks later with a female instructor named Ginny. I liked her instantly. We were the same age and she had a no-nonsense way about her. She was revered by everyone in the local aviation community as an excellent flying instructor. The introductory flight was the most awesome experience of my life! It felt so right to be flying an airplane. She put me through all of the typical maneuvers, with me at the controls! Being up in the air, looking down at earth, gave me a new sense of safety and freedom, and vividly brought back my dreams from childhood about flying out my bedroom window and down the street. When I looked down at roofs of houses, I kept having these déjà vu type of feelings—like I had already done this before. I had never flown an airplane before, and I'd certainly never landed one. But when we began the descent to land the plane, I felt like I had already done this dozens of times. Of course, Ginny was at her controls on the right, and we had a perfect landing, certainly not from my skilled hands. By the time we had taxied the plane to the hangar, I was already "hooked" and ready to sign up for lessons. I didn't care where the money would come from; I was going to learn to fly. *Someday* had arrived!

I began taking flying lessons immediately, and this became the foundation of my new relationship with Jeremy. We began dating at the same time that I started my flying lessons. It was a magical time. I would come home from my flying lessons just floating on air. The adrenaline was so powerful, I lived on it all week! Jeremy was working for the state, also, as a lawyer for the Department of Transportation. I knew a lot of people there and could go over to visit him during the day. Sometimes we would have lunch or walk in the park. We went to contra dances and to plays and to AA meetings together. I had my own sacred meetings, though, that I attended alone. I also attended Al-Anon once a week. I needed balance.

I loved my job with the Office of Substance Abuse and would likely still be in that position today had it not been for a major financial meltdown with the state government. The governor shut down the entire governmental operations for two weeks, and they wiped out hundreds of jobs, mine included. I was "bumped" by another employee who had more seniority than I did.

So I was out of a job. I went to work, again, as a substance abuse counselor for a small agency in Brunswick with a psychologist named David Bellville. He was a wonderful person, and several terrific people were employed at his agency. I had met them all on a licensing visit a few months earlier. I felt honored that he hired me. I began taking courses again at the University of Maine, with a goal of getting my bachelor's degree. One class at a time, though, would take a while.

After a year of dating, Jeremy proposed marriage to me one windy evening at sunset while on a walk in the country. He just stopped, dropped to his knee, took my hand, and asked me to marry him. Wasn't this what every girl wanted? I'm not sure what I felt. I cared deeply for him. But did I love him? I wasn't sure. Did I want to marry him? I wasn't sure. I now had ten years of sobriety. You would think I would know what I wanted by now. My response to him was a stuttering, stammering "W-well, gee—I, ah, okay. Yes, I'll marry you!" We did the engagement ring and the white dress wedding and the whole nine yards, including a Caribbean honeymoon. It was really nice. Really, it was. But, and you know there is a "but," something just wasn't right. When I was walking down the aisle toward him, there was a little voice inside me, nagging me, Don't do it, don't do it. But I didn't listen. I had finally arrived at a place in life where I could be "normal" and I wasn't listening to any stupid nagging voice that might ruin it for me.

For the first few months, the marriage was bliss. He was a good person. He had done some good work in his recovery, had even gone to the Caron Foundation for treatment, and I was proud to be married to him. Jeremy got his pilot's license and took me flying with him.

I continued my flying lessons, and one year to the day from my introductory flight, I was scheduled for my final flight exam. I was so scared I got the hiccups! But my mantra kept me going: I can function while being afraid. I passed the exam that day and became a pilot!

Jeremy and I went flying together all the time, taking turns flying and planning the course. It was really exciting—exhilarating even! I didn't think things could get any better. We took another trip to the Caribbean, and rented a plane and flew around the islands.

My daughter graduated from high school, and her father and his wife came to Maine for the graduation. She was to start at the University of Maine in Augusta in the fall. Things just couldn't be better.

Then, something completely out of my control started happening. I started having nightmares again about men hurting me. I also started having my "water" dreams. I had a dream in which I was swimming in clear, warm Caribbean water and there was a large boat, full of women, who were all calling me to get into the boat with them. It was a nice dream, but I didn't get in the boat, and I didn't understand what it meant. I started having more dreams about women, and now they were becoming sexual.

The next thing that happened knocked me off my track completely. Everywhere I went, I saw penises. Everything—fire hydrants, bananas, telephone poles—everything began to look like phallic to me. I suddenly didn't want to have sexual relations with Jeremy, and I couldn't explain why. He didn't understand at all, and said that if we didn't have sex, it wasn't a marriage—that the marriage was over. I guess I really can't blame him, but I was hoping for his support and understanding. His male ego couldn't take it. I didn't seem to have any control over this, and it was just killing me. How could this happen? I had done all of my work, I had forgiven my father, I had let go of all of the ugliness of my childhood. And now, what the hell was this? It scared me to death.

Around the same time as this began happening, my father came in his motor home to visit, as he had started to do every summer. I didn't want to see him, but I wasn't even sure why. I tried to explain to Jeremy what was happening, leaving out much of the details. He instantly decided the whole thing was wrapped around my incestuous relationship with my father, as I also did. He stated that he didn't want anything to do with my father, and he refused to see him also. At least at this level he was supportive.

One afternoon, my sister Donna was at my house, trying to plan a birthday party for my father and she wanted to know what I was going to bring to eat. I said that we wouldn't be attending. When she asked why, Jeremy answered by saying, "I don't want anything to do with that man because of what he did to Sara." Donna's response was to look at me and say, "Oh, you really have to get over this. It happened a long time ago!" I was outraged, and my old, angry personality kicked in. I yelled at her, "You have no idea what you are talking about. What if it had happened to your daughter? You wouldn't be saying that, would you?" She turned beet red and walked out of the house without saying another word. Needless to say, we didn't attend the birthday party. My interactions between my family and me became tense and almost nonexistent following this. I began to realize that every time I talked to anyone in my family, old thoughts and behaviors would kick in and I felt out of control. I decided to take a break from my family, and wrote a letter to my sisters saying that I didn't want to see them for a while—indefinitely. It was a sad decision to make, and it would prove to have some unfortunate consequences that I came to regret. But there was also a sense of relief. I no longer had to have an adrenaline rush every time the phone rang.

My old friend, suicide, began creeping back into my thoughts. That just devastated me, because I really didn't want to die. Before, when I thought about suicide, and planned it, I didn't carry it through, probably because I was afraid to die. Now I wasn't afraid to die; I just didn't *want* to die anymore. So why, against my own feelings and desires, was this thought process kicking back in again? I knew I needed help, so I sought out therapy with a therapist I knew named Mary Jean Anderson. She was someone I trusted and knew to be compassionate and entirely professional. Once I started talking to her, the idea that I might be a lesbian started to materialize. I knew

I'd had these yearnings on and off for years, but I had always tried to put them aside. Now I was beginning to wonder if this was the direction I was supposed to be going. I still didn't like heterosexual sex. And, with my recent hallucinations about penises all over the place, I didn't want to ever see one again! I did not tell Jeremy any of this. I really didn't want to end my marriage. I wanted to work through this stuff and stay with him. I didn't want to be a lesbian.! But the dreams and hallucinations continued and I felt like I was really slipping a gear.

I was going to more meetings than ever at this point, and also started going to Al-Anon again. I needed balance. I also began to notice that my eating habits were taking on some scary behaviors. I would get up in the night, sneak out to my own kitchen, and quietly make something to eat. I would tiptoe around, usually when I was the only one there. I also began lying about what and when I was eating in order to eat more. For example, I would go to McDonalds and eat a burger and fries on my way somewhere, and then eat dinner with the people I was going to see, and act as though I was hungry. This deceptive, sneaky behavior didn't escape my radar, and I noticed a familiar pattern that I didn't like. I decided to go to Overeaters Anonymous. Darn if I didn't fit right in! Was there anything that *wasn't* wrong with me? But, going to OA not only helped me to get into a healthier eating pattern, but I realized I had been stuffing a lot of feelings and memories down with food, as I had previously done with alcohol.

I began having more periods of dissociation, which began to have a negative impact on my job as a counselor. I would dissociate while working with clients who had similar problems, and I would miss everything they were saying. One day, while we were having a staff meeting, discussing cases, one of the other counselors was talking about families that sleep together, citing a study he had read about in which the children all slept in bed with the parents. I felt myself starting to slide backward down a long tunnel, and the voices of my coworkers seemed to get further and further away. I must have been saying something, but I don't know what. Somebody touched my arm and asked me if I was okay. I kind of snapped out of it and described the long tunnel I was traveling down, and he said, "Oh, you're dissociating. What was it that triggered that to happen?" I was really startled. So this is what dissociation was! I had learned about it, and obviously had been experiencing it all of my life, but never realized it. I began crying and didn't know why. It was frightening because I was in worse shape than most of the patients we were discussing. Once again, I was afraid that I would be sent to a psychiatric hospital and never released! I knew what had triggered it—the conversation about families sleeping together. But I was afraid to say so, so I just made up something, a trick I pulled out of my old habits from childhood. I didn't like doing that, either. It felt like I was losing my recovery.

The only place or time I felt truly safe was in the air, in an airplane, so even though I was emotionally unbalanced, I continued flying. When I was up in the air, looking down at the earth, I felt safer than I had ever felt in my life! I felt the presence of God in the seat beside me and knew that I was doing what I should be doing. Flying is what kept me sane. My mind felt clear and my thinking seemed rational. I talked about it in therapy. And, slowly, something began to materialize that I had never realized. Maybe all those dreams about flying when I was a child weren't dreams at all! I came to believe that they were what some people call "out of body experiences." Maybe I really did fly. How else would I be able to know what the beach on Lake Erie looked like from the air, or the roof of my school? At that point in my life, I had never flown in an airplane! And this explained why, when I began flying lessons, I felt like I had already done this! I *had* done it—many times—only not in an airplane! Those experiences were what saved me during the times of trauma with all those men in my childhood. It seemed rather nice, when I thought about it, like angels were picking me up and carrying me out of the room to save me.

I have worked with patients in my counseling work who would inflict injuries to themselves in reaction to childhood sexual or physical abuse. I have also worked with people who developed serious eating disorders at an early age as a response to these experiences. Other people develop multiple personality disorders in order to escape. To the best of my knowledge, I didn't have multiple personalities or serious eating disorders, nor did I injure myself. I just escaped into the air! The out-of-body flying seemed like a very spiritual way to escape the pain. I dissociated, but I don't believe I changed personalities. I just went somewhere else for a while.

Now that I was beginning to understand these things, I was able to control the dissociative states. When I would feel one coming on, I could pull myself out of it and look around to figure out what the trigger was and then talk myself through it. I came to understand that the body parts that were injured in my childhood still had the memories imbedded in them. Even though, cognitively and spiritually, I let go of the stuff from the past, my body still had the memories. The problem was, now everything was triggering me. All these penises I was seeing would send me reeling. Sadly, I quit my job. I had to. I wasn't doing good work anymore, and I don't think I was good for the clients. I was going to therapy weekly and doing some very difficult work.

"If you are going to describe the truth
leave elegance to the tailor."
—Albert Einstein

CHAPTER 18

another visit to hell

Mary Jean believed that the work I had done previously to let go of my childhood trauma was good, but that I hadn't remembered everything. It made me angry to think that there could be more, and I wondered if this was going to keep happening to me all of my life! Would I ever be free of it? With her help and guidance, I began doing a type of therapy in which you get in touch with your "inner child." I would write in a journal with my non-dominant hand (my left hand), and supposedly what I wrote was from the voice of my child essence, the little girl whom I had left standing on a corner alone all those years ago. She was still waiting for her mommy to come to get her. I realized I had to be the mommy to my little girl. It actually made sense to me. After being instructed by my mother at age six to take care of the rest of the family, it was time I took care of me. But, oh my god, it was difficult work.

I felt like I was regressing back to ten years ago when I first stopped drinking. I was in so much pain I could hardly get up in the morning. The dreams continued to plague me and the penises were everywhere. I just didn't understand it. I wasn't having any vivid memories like I had before—just little flashes once in a while that made no sense at all.

My marriage to Jeremy was dying, and there seemed to be nothing I could do about it. Mary Jean kept encouraging me to talk about the possibility that I was a lesbian, and I didn't want to. But the voices inside me were telling me I had to. She felt it was important that I share this with Jeremy. I didn't want to, because I knew it would be the end of the marriage. I still believed I could work through whatever this was and we could somehow stay married. However, I wasn't getting any support from Jeremy. He was completely focused on the fact that I had stopped having sex with him. To him, the marriage was already over, and he began having an affair with another woman.

In the meantime, I had to have a job. The handwriting was on the wall about my marriage—it would end soon and I couldn't expect any financial support from Jeremy. So I decided to start a business. The flight school where I had learned to fly and where I rented planes asked me to help them with a new, government-mandated drug-testing program for some of the employees. There was a new regulation by the FAA in which all flight instructors, aircraft mechanics, and charter pilots had to have random urine testing for drugs and a plan had to be submitted to the FAA by each small airport in Maine. They wanted to know if I could help them, and after looking at the regulations, I said I would do it. That led to me starting a business in which I did the drug testing for all of the flight base operations in Maine that signed up with my plan. I loved it because I rented an airplane and flew to all of the places where I needed to do urine testing, and I could write the plane rental fees off as a business expense. The other reason this was good for me was that I didn't have to sit in a little room and talk with people about their trauma for an hour at a crack. I just couldn't do that right now. Instead I became a business owner. I discovered entrepreneurship agreed with me. The independence was good for me, and I really didn't have to answer to anyone. However, I barely made enough money to make ends meet. At least I was working and doing something important.

The next thing I did was to take a huge step by talking to one of my women friends whom I knew to be a lesbian. She just smiled and said "welcome." I guess it was assumed that when someone gets so far as to say out loud that they think they are a lesbian, they must be one! I told my friend Barbara. I don't think she understood, but she still loved me and was supportive. Heck, I didn't understand what was happening! How could I expect my friends to understand? My friend Betty also didn't understand, but she was supportive. Her

Catholicism prevented her from truly accepting it, though, and our friendship would suffer as a result of this.

Another friend, Nancy, was a woman whom I had met at an Al-Anon meeting. She had asked me to be her sponsor, and when we began working the steps, it became clear that she was an alcoholic. She painfully accepted this and began going to AA. Our friendship grew from this. When I told her about what I thought about my sexuality, she began crying and admitted that she had been also keeping this secret about herself her whole life, and she, too, thought she was a lesbian. Actually, that didn't come as a surprise to me—I had always thought that about her, but never said anything. So now I had someone to talk to about this business of "coming out." (That's what they call it when people discover they are gay.) I started reading books about homosexuality. They were making sense to me, much to my dismay. One of the books I read—I can't remember the name of it—talked about certain Native American tribes where the adolescents were all given the freedom to make a choice about their sexual identity and who they wanted to mate up with. The idea of having same-gender mates was not taboo. And the women had menstrual huts where they would go and squat over moss on the ground during their menstrual periods. It was warm and dark and safe in the huts and the women had older women for support and wisdom. That culture made so much sense to me.

I also read *Ruby Fruit Jungle* and watched a video called *Desert Hearts*. It started to feel right to me. But, boy, I didn't want it to!

I finally told Jeremy. His initial response was to laugh and make jokes about being married to a dyke. Just one week after I told him, his sister came to visit us from Washington, DC, and stayed a week. We had to make like we were a happy little couple for that week. In a way, I liked it, because I *wanted* to be a happy little couple. I didn't want any of this to be happening. But when she left, Jeremy made quick plans to leave, and a few days later, I came home to find all of his things gone. He had left and wouldn't be coming back. I wondered if he had moved in with his new girlfriend. Once again, I felt like I had been kicked in the gut. I felt like I was failing at everything all over again!

Painfully, I talked to my daughter about it. She didn't understand, and began to cry. But her response was, "You're my mom, and I love you and nothing can change that. I just don't understand." It felt horrible to have to tell her this stuff. I wanted her to have a normal mom, not an oddball! I think she wanted a normal mom, too. I really couldn't explain much to help her understand. I didn't understand it myself.

Shortly after this conversation with Jenni, she came home one evening, sat on the edge of my bed, and tearfully told me that the young man she was dating had confessed to her that he thought he was gay. Jenni wanted me to explain this to her. I was pleased that she considered me someone she could ask about this, but I didn't have a lot of answers for her. I did, however, give him the names of two young gay men I knew who were willing to talk to him. Jenni was brokenhearted. She thought it was something she had done wrong. I assured her that was not the case at all. I was relieved to learn that she had never had intercourse with him, so she didn't have to worry about the possibility of STDs (rather presumptuous on my part). It seemed somewhat ironic that this would happen to her at this time. Was this really part of God's plan for me after all? I didn't want it to be.

I began to go out to dinner with some of the women in the gay community. And I went to a wellness conference for women. I distinctly remember, while listening to a speaker, the feeling that came over me when all of the women at the conference began to laugh. The sound of women's laughter, the absence of men's voices, felt so wonderful. Being with just women seemed somehow safe to me, and the images of penises were fading. But I was still having serious nightmares and I was depressed and was dissociating a lot. I continued my therapy with Mary Jean, and did my non-dominant hand journaling faithfully. It was kind of weird. Whenever I sat down to do this writing, it was though I was sent back in time to my childhood, my early childhood, before the death of my mother. Bits and pieces of memories from when I was three years old began to surface, such as the time I fell down and hit my forehead on the corner of the cement steps. I remember seeing blood pouring out of my head, I remember the pain and fear, and I remember seeing my mother, the nurse, standing in the front doorway with my sister Joyce in her arms. The next thing I remember was sitting on my father's lap, in the passenger side of someone's car. I was bleeding all over my father's white T-shirt and I remember saying to him, "Don't cry, Daddy, it doesn't hurt." I remember lying in the hospital emergency room, staring up at a big, round, very bright light, and I could see the needle and thread as they stitched up my head. I heard a huge commotion and discovered that my mother, who had finally arrived at the hospital, was making a scene because they wouldn't let her in the room where I was being treated. I finally got to see her, and she was crying, and again I said, "Don't cry, Mommy, it doesn't hurt." What a little toughie I was then! Was I taking care of my parents at age three?

In my non-dominant hand journal, I began writing things that didn't make sense to me, like I was having a conversation with someone I couldn't see. It was scary and painful, but I didn't know why. Back in our house in Ashtabula, when I was three, I had a little secret place I went to in the backyard. There were tall grasses, I don't know what they were called. But, at age three, they were taller than me, and I would go in there and make a little nest for myself and hide. Some of these memories began to surface through my journal writing. And then I got out some crayons (from my daughter's old toy box) and drew a picture with my left hand. I don't know what possessed me to draw the picture, or where it came from. What appeared when I was finished was a picture of a little girl with red hair, sitting on her knees in the tall grass, with her pants pulled down! Her face looked sad and hurt. This shook me to the bone, and I had to make an emergency call to my therapist, something I had never done before then. I went into see her, and the more I talked about the picture, more memories began to surface. I recalled having a problem, at age three, of pooping my pants. I can remember it vividly, feeling how good it felt to get it out of me. But my mother saw what had happened, and rubbed my nose in the poop. I swear the smell of feces was in my nose for ten years! It was absolutely dehumanizing. I felt like an animal.

But the question came up in therapy, "Why was I doing that at age three?" What had happened to trigger something like that? I was long past being potty trained. I didn't know. But I would find out, whether I wanted to or not.

I continued my non-dominant hand journaling. It sent me into a deep depression and for a short period of time, I was agoraphobic. I was afraid to go out of my house, to see people, afraid to even talk to people. The only place I went during the span of one week was to my therapist. Then, my neighbor, Jane, called me and asked if I would take care of her cat for a week while she and her husband went on vacation. She said that in return for taking care of the cat, I could have the keys to her cabin at a lake nearby. I could even take the cat to the cabin, because he was accustomed to going there. This sounded like heaven on earth to me, and I agreed, enthusiastically.

The cabin was just a little Maine "camp," rustic and full of old, chipped dishes, sagging beds with old quilts, with no television, and situated on a small lake about twenty-five minutes from my house. It was secluded enough that I never had to see another human being, except for someone in a boat, the whole time I was there. I took my guitar and my journal. I would use this time to heal and begin recovery, from what I wasn't sure. But I was tired of this awful mental/spiritual place I was in, and it didn't seem like I was going to figure out exactly what I was going through. I cooked myself decadent meals, which I ate out on the deck. I took early morning swims in the chilly water, before anyone else was moving, and long walks in the woods during the day. At night I lit a candle and played my guitar and sang. One night, I put the guitar down and felt the presence of something or someone. I can't really describe it. It was a safe, warm feeling. I just stared at the candle for a long time, and a memory began to surface from age three. I didn't want that to happen—that was the farthest thing from my mind. But there it was, nonetheless, this ugly reality bubbling to the surface of my mind.

The memory involved a penis and my anus. I don't know whose penis, but I do not believe it was my father. It was possibly a young man whom my parents often had babysit for us. When it came to me what it probably meant, I felt like someone had put a stick of dynamite inside of me. I just simply fell apart. A hoard of emotions came surging forth, and I thought I was going to vomit up my entire insides. The sobs that erupted came from way down deep inside of me—from my anus! They came up through my body and out my mouth. Words cannot describe what I felt, and I truly thought I had slipped over the edge, finally, and, if I didn't kill myself, I would be put away forever. I tried to call my therapist, through the answering service, because by now it was the middle of the night, only to discover that she was away on vacation. I would have to do this alone. The "presence" was still there with me, and I sought it out for comfort. Could it have been God, an angel, my mother? I didn't know. But someone or something was there with me, else how could I have gotten through that night alive?

I went into the bathroom and took a hot, cleansing bath, scrubbing so hard, I thought I'd take the skin off. I had to wash away the pain, the toxins that had been with me for so long, and the filth, shame, and guilt! If I could have scrubbed my insides, I would have. I watched as the water drained out of the tub, feeling as though I was watching a terrible, destructive tornado blow away and disappear, leaving me limp, but alive. Then I scoured the tub thoroughly, and put the plug in the drain so the toxins wouldn't come back up! I hoped that it didn't drain into the lake. I know this was going a little over the edge, but I couldn't sleep if I didn't do that.

And sleep I did, because, for the first time in my life, I felt clean, and I was completely exhausted. It was sort of like when you have the flu and when you finally can vomit up the germs, you feel better. My sleep was full of rambling nightmares and dreams that were disconnected and frightful. But the last dream I had before morning was a dream of swimming in beautiful, clear Caribbean waters, just floating out in the middle of the sea, looking back at the beach where there were huge boulders scattered around, some huddled together, making caves that the water flowed into with each wave. No one was around and it was okay and I wasn't scared. I could see to the bottom as clear as I could see the sun and clouds. I decided to dive down below the surface and discovered I could breathe underwater! It was like I had a secret place to go where no one else could go. I woke up feeling strong and cleansed. But when I went to get up and go about my day, I found I could barely move. I discovered I had developed a crop of hemorrhoids so big I couldn't even put my legs together, or even sit down. I had never had hemorrhoids in my life, and I could think of only one thing that would cause them: my memories from last night. The body parts carry the memories, and they hadn't forgotten! What a cruel thing to have happen. But maybe it was the final bit of toxin coming out of me, the stuff I couldn't scrub away.

I had to call Jeremy to take me to the emergency room. It was a humiliating and embarrassing experience. I couldn't stop crying, and I just couldn't explain to the hospital staff what was wrong with me. I just wanted them to help me treat the hemorrhoids. Why they didn't call in a psychiatric consultation, I'll never know. But as the hemorrhoids began to heal, so did I. I closed up the camp, took the cat, and went home. I felt like I was entering my house on a new spiritual plane.

I went home and approached life with a new vigor. I noticed as I was driving home that the objects that had looked like penises were now their old selves. What a relief! That paranoid feeling of foreboding had left me, and I felt my unit of worth filling up another notch.

Back on the therapy couch, feeling like a different person, I asked Mary Jean if she thought my flying had anything to do with all of this. After a period of thoughtful silence, she said, "Do you believe in out-of-body experiences?" My mind went back to my childhood and the flying dreams—of flying out my window and seeing the roof of my school. "Is that what I did? Did I really fly? Is that possible? People will really think I'm crazy if I tell anyone this."

Mary Jean responded, "Out-of-body experiences are a form of dissociation—a very spiritual way of escaping the pain and fear of the type of trauma you experienced. Not everyone believes in it, but I do. And, in your case, I believe that is what happened. The beautiful thing is, you have now taken it three hundred and sixty degrees by becoming a pilot. You can fly! It is just wonderful what you have done."

This explained why I felt so much safer up in the air than on the ground with people. It also explained why I thought I had already learned to fly when I was taking lessons. It explained the déjà vu feelings when I flew. It put it all together for me. Now, after my week at the lake, I had another chapter to add to the childhood trauma experiences.

As my therapy continued, I realized I had to do something to let go of this new piece of my childhood. I felt such a sense of relief after my experiences at the cabin at the lake that it seemed I could get beyond this. The fear that had overtaken me was gone. I decided to write my experiences into a fairy tale, so I could close it like a book and put it on a shelf. I wouldn't throw it away. I just wanted the option to have it up on a shelf instead of carrying it around with me all the time. I had heard about this from someone who had been to a professional workshop. It seemed like just the right way for me to move on. Here is my fairy tale.

Sephonie

The Girl Who Could Fly

Once upon a time, in a land far, far away, in a town near a beautiful lake, there were a man and a woman. The man had just come back from the other side of the ocean after fighting in a terrible war, and he was sad and lonely. The woman was very sad because the man she had loved died fighting in the terrible war. Out of their loneliness, they found each other and fell instantly in love. They got married right away. Soon, they had a beautiful baby girl with red hair, sparkling blue eyes, and a splash of freckles across her face. Her mother thought she was very special and named her "Sephonie," after the mythical goddess Persephone.

Sephonie grew to be very musical, and she could often be seen and heard all alone in the tall grasses in the garden singing softly to herself.

Sephonie's parents went on to have two more daughters.

Her mother was so happy for she wanted to fill her house with children. But, alas, one sad, dark day, she died trying to have a fourth child.

Sephonie's father was so terribly brokenhearted and lonely that he started drinking a magic potion to make him forget about his wife. But whenever he drank the potion, he turned into a terrible monster and scared Sephonie and her sisters.

Sephonie, being the oldest child, was given much work to do in her mother's absence. Often Sephonie's mother would come to visit her in her sleep to help her with her chores. Sephonie would talk to her about her father, and her mother told her she had to take care of him since she was the oldest girl. One night, when her father was drinking the magic potion, he thought Sephonie was his dead wife. He forced her to lie down with him and then he raped her. It hurt Sephonie a lot and she was very scared. It began to happen many times, and Sephonie found that she could do something magic to keep from feeling the pain and fear. She found that she could make her spirit leave her body and fly. She would fly around the room and out the window, then fly over the buildings and along the roads and beaches. It was wonderful!

It seemed that drinking the magic potion and turning into a monster was something that ran in her father's family. Her grandfather and her uncles also turned into monsters. And when they did, they also did things to hurt Sephonie. So, every time it happened, she would make her spirit leave her body and fly away.

Sephonie started having dreams of being all alone in a dark, violent sea with high, crashing waves. The dreams scared her so much that she was often afraid to go to sleep. She began to have dreams during the day about killing her father, and she was so afraid someone would find out that she didn't make very many friends. She had three special friends who loved her. But she couldn't tell them her secrets, and it separated her from them. She was so alone.

One day, when Sephonie was alone praying in church, she met a prince. He was the most handsome man she had ever known. His name was Richard. She knew from the moment she met him that she was in love with him. He, too, fell in love with Sephonie, for he thought she was the most lovely girl he had ever seen. They were too young to get married, so they courted. Prince Richard was so very kind to Sephonie. He never hurt her and always protected her. She felt like she was in heaven whenever she was with him. But one night she had a dream about her wedding. She dreamed she was in her white wedding dress walking toward the waiting Prince Richard, when she looked down and saw that her dress was torn and soiled. When she woke up, she knew what it meant. It meant that her marriage to Prince Richard would be tarnished and that she was not to marry him. But she did not tell him about the dream. She wanted to marry him more than anything in the world, but she knew it wouldn't happen. After the dream, she was cruel to him and chased him out of her life.

Sephonie was very sad after that, and nobody ever heard her singing in the garden anymore. She began to drink the magic potion to try to forget her loneliness and broken heart. Her friend Rebecca had gone away across the sea. Sephonie felt completely alone in the world. So, one day, when she was almost grown up, she packed some clothes and ran away to a promised land of milk and honey, where there was always sunshine and where the mountains met the sea, never to return to her home. There, she met another prince named John. He was tall, dark, and handsome. He told Sephonie that he loved her and wanted her for his wife. Sephonie married him and they had a beautiful daughter. But Sephonie continued to have the terrible dreams and continued to drink the magic potion. Sometimes she turned into a monster herself. She took her daughter and ran away to the dry, barren desert and tried to escape the dreams. But they followed her. So she continued to drink the magic potion.

Sephonie was very sad and lonely. Her beautiful daughter was her only reason for living. Her mother never visited her in her dreams anymore, and she couldn't seem to make herself fly to escape. She was too far away to talk to her childhood friends. So she ran and ran. She and her daughter found themselves in another land far away, near another sea, where the world was frozen and very different. But the dreams continued. The magic potion didn't work anymore, but she found that no matter how hard she tried, she couldn't stop drinking it. It was now poison to her, and it was killing her!

One cold winter's night, while the snow blew outside the cabin she lived in, Sephonie felt she could no longer stand the terrible dreams and loneliness. She tried to take her own life. However, just as she was about to do it, a bright light— bright as a million sunrises—came into her room. A voice told her to go to see a wonderful, white-haired fairy queen who would help her. Sephonie was so surprised and taken aback by the light and the voice that she did not take her own life. The next day, she went and found the fairy queen who helped her to stop drinking the magic potion. For twenty-eight days, she was banished to a special place and then came home to meet with the fairy queen. The fairy queen told her she loved her and Sephonie realized that it had been a very long time since anyone had told her that. Being loved meant that she could believe in hope for happiness. She learned that she could get rid of the dreams by giving them to the fairy queen every time they came to her. And the fairy queen could magically make them go away.

The fairy queen told her that if she wanted, she could fly. This was different from the flying she did when she was younger. This time, she found that she could *actually* fly! She didn't have to make her spirit l eave her body. She took her body with her and flew like a bird! It was so wonderful that Sephonie knew she would never drink the magic potion again. She knew that now that she could fly, she could do anything, and that no one could ever hurt her again.

So, if you're out singing in your garden and you think you see a redheaded maiden flying in and out of the clouds, take a closer look. It will probably be Sephonie.

The End

I chose the goddess Persephone because she was described in mythical stories as a carefree girl who gathered flowers and played with her friends when Hades in his chariot suddenly appeared out of a vent in the earth, took the screaming maiden by force, and carried her back to the underworld to be his unwilling bride. She was raped by the devil! That certainly fit my life!

It helped me immensely to write this story. I could look at my life from a different perspective, like it had happened to someone else, and I could, in fact, close it and put it up on a shelf, free to take it down anytime I wished.

I was still developing my business, and I jumped into it with both feet. I decided to try to bid for drug testing jobs for other companies, such as the railroad industry and the Maine Yankee nuclear energy plant, owned by Central Maine Power. I had heard that they did aggressive, mandatory random urine drug testing on all of their employees. As I began collecting the data I needed for these bids, I learned that in order to bid on any of these big jobs, I would have to purchase a type of liability insurance, called Errors and Omissions Insurance. It would cover my business and me if I should make a simple error on the detailed paperwork required by the federal government on drug testing, which might result in a test to be considered invalid. That could be disastrous if the test were to come back positive. It would mean that an employee could be walking around with drugs in his blood, but the urine test would be invalid and the employee could keep on working. After shopping for insurance, I met with an insurance broker, who searched, literally, the world for insurance that would cover what the Feds wanted. It would cost me a small fortune, and even then, the only company that would cover me sent a proposed policy with fifteen pages of exclusions. I asked the broker how other companies did this, and he said it had to do with credentials. He said, "I could sell you almost the same type of insurance for only $350 per year if you were a registered nurse!" I just stared at him. I had been seriously considering returning to school to finish my degree, but I didn't know what direction to go. Nursing was something that had been one of my dreams when I was a child, but I had thrown that out like the baby with the bathwater long ago. Now I was at a new crossroads in my life and the idea seemed to have new meaning to me. The diversity in a nursing career meant I could probably go anywhere and always find a job. It also meant I would never get bored with my work.

I went home to think this through. And then I went over to the University of Maine at Augusta and talked with my friend, Beth Clark, who was an assistant dean of the school of nursing there. She looked at my school transcript and recommended that I go to the University of Southern Maine in Portland and get my baccalaureate degree in nursing, since I had already done so much coursework. She said that the field of nursing was changing and that a four-year degree was going to carry much more weight in the coming years. It would result in higher salaries and more career opportunities. This gave me a lot of thinking to do. I didn't want to commute daily to Portland to go to school. But did I want to sell my house and move there? I began to think about my mother, who had been a nurse, and I wondered what she would say if she were here. My head was spinning.

I continued my therapy with Mary Jean. Clearly I had made a major breakthrough and could now begin the process of letting go of the stuff that had been plaguing me my whole life. It explained so much—why I had this boiling rage inside of me that wouldn't go away. It explained why I yelled all the time—to be heard! It was as though the little girl inside had never felt heard, and the only way I felt I even existed was if I could be heard through yelling. I obviously didn't think about this every time I opened my mouth. But now, working it through with Mary Jean, it began to make sense. My friend Barbara had once told me that at meetings when we said the Lord's Prayer, I said it so loud that she felt she didn't have to say it at all. I said it loud enough for everyone! I would learn to talk softer. But that would take a lot of work and a lot of time. It also explained why, after ten years of sobriety and doing all of the work I had done on my childhood trauma, I continued to have periods of dissociation. I wondered if I would no longer have them now.

But there was still this business of my sexual orientation to be dealt with. After my recent revelation, I could understand why I had these yearnings for women. But I really didn't want to act on them right now. It seemed safe to not be in any kind of relationship at the present time. I decided to put it on hold. I didn't have to run out and have sex with someone! So I worked on developing my business and looked into going to nursing school. I was finding a fresh new direction in my life. This seemed good.

The University of Southern Maine accepted me into their nursing school and transferred all of my credits from UMA and Kent State! So now the dilemma was whether or not to stay in my house or sell it and move to Portland.

Jeremy filed for divorce right away, and began telling me he wanted his share of equity from my house. I had lived there for ten years, and he was there with me a total of one and a half years. It didn't seem fair, but I guess divorces are never fair. I hired my old boss Roger as my attorney.

I decided to sell my house and make a fresh start. I had always been disappointed in Augusta as a place to live, and Portland seemed like an exciting place to start my life over. This could end a chapter in my life and be the start of another one. As I began the business of getting ready to sell my house and move, my therapy with Mary Jean was also drawing to a close. I would miss talking to her. She was so safe and caring and understanding. Just before I moved away, Mary Jean asked me if I would take her flying! Talk about trust! She had a twelve-year-old son who was interested in becoming a pilot, and she thought this would be a good way to introduce him to the world of flying. We picked a nice, warm, sunny day, and we rented the more expensive plane that had some nicer features and flew faster than the ones I usually rented. We took off and flew over the Kennebec River, and out into the country. We did a couple of dips over their house.

Mary Jean was scared to death, but she never said a word. She sat in the backseat and took pictures. Her son sat in the front and just beamed from ear to ear the whole time, asking nonstop questions. It was good for all of us, and a fitting ending to my therapy with Mary Jean. I would really miss her. But I could take with me the new me that had emerged while I was in therapy with her. I left the old me with her, to be put in the closed case. I also left with her my non-dominant hand journaling and pictures. I didn't want to be tempted to keep reading them and trigger old feelings and memories again. They were too painful. I had done my work, and it was time to move on. Those were mementos of the past I could do without.

I sold my house for a decent profit. But I didn't get the money since I had financed my home through Farmer's Home, a federally funded program that sets aside interest for low-income home buyers and then gets a huge payback when the house is sold. They had subsidized my interest each month (which was 10¾ percent) over the past ten years so that I could afford the payments. But it was no deal. I had to pay it all back when I sold the house. Every penny. So at the closing, even though I sold the house for about $40,000 more than I owed on it, I only received a check for $8,000. With it I paid the back taxes, my divorce lawyer's fees, and my daughter's first semester at UMA. What was left I used to pay for my own first semester at USM. I had no money. I couldn't even buy another house in Portland, which had been part of my plan. But I was assured by an accountant that since I had paid all of that money in mortgage interest, I would be able to claim it on my income tax return and would get a handsome return in the spring. This seemed okay to me, and I could make do until then. I had my business for income, and I would find a rental situation that I could afford and still go to school. After the first semester, I would qualify for student loans. One day at a time!

Going to school meant setting goals and figuring out how to meet them, something I had never been able to accomplish. I didn't know how. I realized this one day while having lunch with a former coworker, Jim. He was talking about how he and his family had been planting fruit trees over the weekend. His kids helped him decide what kind of trees to plant, and helped him dig the holes.

He said they felt a deep sense of satisfaction after patting down the earth around the spindly little leafless trees. I asked him how long it would be before they bear fruit. He said, "Oh, three or four years at least, maybe longer."

I stared at him in amazement. "Why on earth would you want to plant something that will take that long to grow? You might not even be there when the first fruit appears."

He just cocked his head and said, "So what? That's not the point. They'll be here for someone else, even perhaps my children and their children. Isn't that what's important?"

I realized that I didn't know what was important. I had always considered my life temporary. Growing up with alcoholics, I had learned never to count on anything. I never knew if I would be around tomorrow, let alone next spring, or three years from now. The idea of planting a tree and expecting to be around to see the fruit was not within my realm of understanding. I sat there, hoping he wouldn't notice my eyes filling with tears. How lucky his kids were to grow up never being afraid of a rug being pulled out from under them, that they didn't have to live in constant fear of being hit or watching helplessly while one of their treasured possessions was taken away or destroyed as a measure of parental control, or that they might be, once again, whisked off to another place to live.

Fruit trees! What a concept. My thoughts wandered to my daughter, with whom I had never been able to share this value. I realized that I had always planted annuals every spring, subconsciously believing there was a good chance we wouldn't be around the next spring. That we, the greater We, would not be here. I had no concept of why we lived or died. To me, life was only the here and now. Everyone I had loved had either hurt me, left me, or died. What right did I have to live? Why did anyone live? Why would I want to plant something that would have no reason to live? I talked to some friends about this, and a new concept began to develop for me: that all things on earth are living, all are part of what makes up the whole of life—just for us. And our lives are just simply to live, to feel, to experience passion, and to love; to experience the awesome miracle of birth, the beauty of a sunrise or a spring flower opening, and to taste luscious fruit. I learned that it is up to each of us to keep planting trees, no matter what our life situation is, so that someone who may walk this path tomorrow will experience the miracle of rebirth, the fragrance of blossoms, and the nourishment of fruit. I learned that life is really quite precious. It's temporary and short, and we only get to do it once. So I planted some tulip and daffodil bulbs in my garden before I left my little house. I vowed I would plant bulbs or trees wherever I lived, and I would start giving them away for gifts.

I said good-bye to my house, each room, one at a time. We had a good ten years, my house and me. We recovered together, and we were both in better shape than we had started out. I thanked the house for the spirit and energy it had given me, and, with a tear rolling down my cheek, I walked out and closed the door. One major chapter in my life closed—another was about to begin.

For the first time in many, many years, I was no longer thinking about suicide.

"Let choice whisper in your ear
and love murmur in your heart.
Be ready.
Here comes life."
— Maya Angelou

CHAPTER 19

midlife crisis management

My first class at USM in the fall semester of 1993 was on a hot day, and I sat at my desk with sweat literally dripping off my face onto my papers. But when I looked around, I realized that no one else was sweating. I was having hot flashes, made worse by stress. At forty-six I was starting menopause. I knew this process had begun—how appropriate that this would happen just as I was discovering so many things about myself as a woman! I did a lot of reading about menopause and decided it would be a liberating experience, and so I preferred to call the hot flashes "power surges." But my attitude didn't help the night sweats and sleep deprivation. How would I ever be able to study if I couldn't sleep! Since I had gone to Overeater's Anonymous, I had decided to become a semi-vegetarian, and I tried to eat only organic and natural foods. I wanted to go through menopause in a natural way, without having to take hormones made from horse urine! But eventually the sleep deprivation got the best of me. I would just be wasting my time and money if I couldn't concentrate and study. I gave in and went to a doctor and was put on hormone replacement therapy. Within a week, I felt alive again! I continued my vegetarianism and began doing yoga, jogging around the Back Cove and walking around Portland at night. My body was in terrific shape, and I figured my mind would also be.

I scraped together enough money to take another trip to the

Caribbean during the Christmas semester break. My friend Nancy and I went together to Maho Bay in St. Johns, in the Virgin Islands. I had been there once before, and I loved it. While we were there, we spent a day on Virgin Gorda, one of the British-owned islands in the chain. It was a magical, spiritual place. At the far end of the island, there is a beach called the Baths with large, ancient-looking boulders, some of which form caves in which the tide forms pools or "baths." When I stood on that beach, I suddenly realized that it was the beach in the dream I had when I was in the little cabin on the lake the previous summer. I couldn't believe it! Despite the large waves and strong surf, I felt compelled to swim out beyond the breakers and look back at the beach, just as I had done in my dream. Nancy didn't think it was a good idea because of the undertow, but I went out anyway. I'm really not much of a swimmer, and practically, it wasn't a smart move. But I felt so drawn to it and I believed I would be safe. I swam out beyond the breakers and turned around and just stayed there, treading water and looking at the boulders on the beach. They were exactly as they had been in my dream. It was a very powerful experience. There was an incredible spiritual pull on that beach—I can't describe it. Although, as in the dream, I could see to the bottom, I did not dive down to see if I could breathe underwater. I knew that would not be possible. But the experience of being out there and looking back at the beach was enough for me. I wanted to stay on that beach forever! The metaphor of "the baths" seemed to fit the experiences I had been through. The message it gave me was that I was on the right path in my life's journey. When the trip was over, we came home to a terrible snowstorm that pretty much wiped out all of the magic of the vacation. But I will never forget that beach.

Following that trip, Nancy and I developed a "relationship"—a lesbian relationship. I have to say that the experience was extremely healing for me. It enabled me to experience myself as a sexual/sensual human being without the presence of a penis. I never could develop this part of myself because I was either intoxicated or filled with dread whenever I was in a sexual situation. Now it was safe for me to develop into a mature, sensual, and functioning woman. But I still didn't *want* to be a lesbian. The relationship lasted for about a year, and then I ended it. I didn't love her the way she wanted to be loved, and I couldn't seem to fit into the lesbian lifestyle. I am afraid my ending the relationship hurt Nancy a lot, and for that, I am regretful. But I am not regretful that I had the experience.

Back in school in January, I met a woman named Merilyn who was my age and had left her home in Cape Elizabeth to start nursing school. We quickly became good friends, and we walked and talked and studied together. She made it clear that she was one hundred percent heterosexual, which was a great relief to me. It was fun to have a friend who thought I was a normal person. We had similar personalities, in that we were very intense and direct. We both were very serious about nursing school, and we helped each other study and work on our projects and papers. We were both broke most of the time, so we spent a lot of time walking the streets of Portland at night, which I found to be just delightful. Since Portland is situated on the oceanfront, there is always a fresh ocean breeze and the sounds of gong buoys and ferry boats always in the background. The harbor is full of hustle and bustle, with people from all corners of the earth coming in and out of the city on large ships. My drug-testing business took me out onto some of those ships to do random testing of the crews. It was kind of exciting and offered a diversion from the grueling work of nursing school. I was called to do the drug testing when a large oil tanker slammed into the Portland bridge and spilled thousands of gallons of oil into the harbor. I was on TV for about twenty seconds!

In the spring, after collecting the data to file my income tax return, I received a huge blow. I learned that I could not claim the $23,000 in back interest I had paid at my real estate closing, because it was no longer considered interest. Since the Farmer's Home Administration had "subsidized" it for me, they paid the interest, and it was now called "subsidy," not interest. They got the tax credit. On top of this, I got socked with capital gains tax on the amount of money I would have made in profit from my house, but that I had to pay back to Farmer's Home. So I now owed the Internal Revenue Service more than $8,000 and my state tax department $3,000 and I had no money! I would never be able to buy a house. I sat down and wept until I had no more tears. Why did I always have to pay so dearly for my mistakes?

I went to work in a per-diem counseling position at Mercy Hospital in their alcohol and drug Recovery Center. There, I could get the hours I needed to balance with my school schedule. It worked out well. Mercy seemed like a good employer, and I liked the program. The medical director was Dr. Evans., my doctor from when I went to alcoholism treatment in 1981. It seems I had come full circle!

School was very hard for me. I had never learned how to study, and I would have to teach myself some ground rules in order to make it work. I lived from one class to the next. And I always knew that I only had get through semesters, not lifetimes of difficulty. Each semester got a little easier because I learned how to do it more efficiently.

I took a yoga class offered at USM and began practicing yoga at night before going to bed. I would do yoga for about forty-five minutes, sit and meditate, and then take a long, hot bath with candlelight. After that I went to bed. It helped to shed the stress and anxiety of each day. Somewhere along this time, my meditation began to take on a different twist. I began using self-guided meditation in which I had an image of myself walking along a beach, toward an old cottage sitting on the rocks. I would walk up to the house and enter through the back door, where the lights were on. I would walk through the house into the living room, where a fire was in the fireplace and an elderly woman was sitting in a chair, drinking a cup of tea, waiting for me. She was lovely, with long graying/blond hair, and she was wearing a loosely fitting blouse and skirt. She had incredibly bright blue eyes and a warm voice. I would sit and talk with this wise old woman and get answers to some of my questions about how to handle the situations in my life. I came to realize that this old woman was me—me as an old, wise woman. I was getting advice from myself!

I have no idea how this meditative experience manifested itself, but I practiced it throughout nursing school, and it was like having my own personal spiritual guide. I can no longer find this place or the woman when I meditate, even when I try to, and I miss her and our conversations. She was there for me when I needed her.

During my last year at school, I began questioning whether or not I really was a lesbian. I began volunteering for the Maine Lesbian and Gay Political Alliance, with the goal of meeting people like me. They ended up asking me to be on the board of directors. The longer I stayed on that board, the more I began to question my sexuality. Maybe what I was questioning was whether I wanted to be part of this culture. It seemed as though most of the gay people I met centered their whole identity around being gay, and their social life was focused only on other gay people. I couldn't adhere to that. I had too many other interests and friends in the "straight world" to abandon it for this cause. Could I be bisexual? Was that really me?

I took a trip to see Dick Forringer in North Carolina. Then, while I was still in nursing school, he went on a sabbatical and attended Fordham University in New York City to get his master's degree in education. I went to see him a lot. We had fun in the neutrality of the Big Apple, and a new romance began to form. We started talking about the possibility of living together. We thought we might start a whole new life together when we both graduated. I was forty-eight and he was fifty-one, but we still had a lot of life left to live.

However, as the talk about cohabitating approached becoming a reality, Dick began to back off. He was truly afraid of commitment, and as it turned out, he didn't really want to settle down with anyone. I suspect that he was a little uncomfortable with my dual sexual identity. And I think he wanted someone who could be his "out-of-town fun-time girl," someone he would go with to the Caribbean, meet in the city, go to fly with in Osh Kosh, Wisconsin (he was training to be a pilot, too), but not someone to live with. That was clearly not what I wanted. To me it felt like prostitution, or like being a mistress. I wanted no part of it. So just a couple of months before I graduated from USM, I sent him a letter saying as much and basically ending our plans, or what I though were our plans. I had been feeling a tugging inside that he would never really follow through with the plan of living together. So that was over, once and for all. It took me all those years to realize that we actually had very little in common. He was a sports enthusiast—no, a sports addict. He watched every sports event on TV. He played golf several times a week. The décor in his house was all black—masculine. He ate nothing but junk food. He had very poor communication skills and had an outrageous fear of going to doctors—hence he never went. What had I seen in him? I realized that the relationship I had with him in the sixties was based on my needing an angel to rescue me from my father, and he filled the bill quite nicely. I mistook that for deep, undying love. In actuality, it was desperate codependency. It served its purpose at the time, but it wouldn't work now. I do still care deeply for him. Despite my negative narrative of his life, he is a wonderful person, an astounding math teacher who loves his students and will make someone else a terrific mate. And because we have known each other since childhood, I will always consider him a special friend—actually, like family. But lovers? No.

Just days after I sent the letter to Dick, the city of Portland was inundated with a terrible nor'easter. It was October 1996. Three storms converged together over the Atlantic, and we got walloped. I was living in a little apartment over a garage in Westbrook, right next to the Presumscot River. The storm caused several dams to break along the river, and the river overflowed its banks and many people in the neighborhood, including me, were forced to evacuate. The entire house was flooded, and a large portion of my belongings were destroyed. Some of the things I lost were mementos of my mother that I had been carrying around all of my life. It broke my heart. I guess these things happen to people all the time, but it caused me a lot of grief, right at a time when I didn't need it.

I graduated with honors from USM Nursing School in December 1996, and was honored to give the graduation speech. My friend Merilyn, who had graduated the semester before me, put my nursing pin on me in the ceremony. I used my mother's nursing pin that I had held on to all these years. It was quite a moving moment for me. At forty-eight, I was the oldest in my class. It left me exhausted and extremely depressed. Going to nursing school and experiencing menopause at the same time is not highly recommended! I had to work very hard to do well.

I began to worry about my daughter, who was in a relationship with an abusive, alcoholic man. She still lived in Augusta and hadn't finished college. She was working as a waitress and having major struggles with relationships. I knew it was because of poor role modeling on my part and my basic lack of parenting skills. I couldn't shake my guilt.

My sisters and I had not spoken to each other for three years. I had tried to make a connection with my sister, Donna, but I was shut down with a cruel, nasty letter from her saying she was glad I was out of her life and that she didn't miss me. She said she didn't want anything to do with me. I had seen my father once for about fifteen minutes the previous summer, when he was on his way in his motor home back to Texas, where they had settled into their retirement home. My other sister, Joyce, however, came to my graduation. None of them knew what I had been through, and they probably would never know. It seemed they really didn't care. I didn't matter to them anymore. I learned much later that my sisters had both been through some really tough situations as well during the three years of incommunicado—and I hadn't been there to support them. I had been pretty self-centered in my quick exodus from my family. Now, I had a new life that no one could take away from me. Would I get the chance to reconcile with my family? I didn't know. At this point, all I could think of was passing the State Nursing Boards.

I studied very, very hard for the Board exam, and I passed it on the first attempt. I applied for three jobs and was offered all three of them. I chose to work at Mercy in the newly formed Women's Surgical Unit. I was told that all nurses must have at least one year of medical-surgical experience before they could go on to specialize in anything else. I had no idea of the new challenges that would lie ahead of me. I had been warned that "Nurses eat their young" and I was about to find out what that meant!

"The greatest glory in living lies
not in never failing,
but in rising every time we fall."
—Nelson Mandela

CHAPTER 20

i'm a nurse

In March 1997, I began working in the Women's Surgical Unit at Mercy Hospital as a full-time nurse. My orientation felt like I was being thrown to the wolves with everyone teaching me, and no one teaching me. No one was actually assigned to orient me or be my mentor. I was staffed as an extra for two weeks so I could get my sea legs, but it was excruciatingly hard. Being tired and depressed didn't help me any. It was assumed that because I had just graduated with a four-year degree in nursing, I should already know how to be a nurse. But the reality was, I had received only the minimal amount of clinical experience in nursing school. They had focused on the academic rather than the clinical experience. I had no idea what I was getting myself into. And these nurses seemed to resent me. I was older than them, and they had fifteen years' experience on me. I was like a deer in the headlights for the first three months I worked there. Why no one died on my shift, I'll never know. I was not a good nurse, and I became more and more depressed as the weeks passed. I couldn't keep up with the duties assigned to me. I worked the evening shift, and every evening I was there long past my shift trying to catch up on my duties and paperwork. It seemed I was always doing something wrong, and I felt like I hadn't learned anything in school. The student loans were about to come due, and I was questioning what in God's name I had done to myself. I was scared all the time.

In May, Merilyn had a terrible accident. She had a severe

anaphylactic reaction to a black fly sting and was in serious condition in Maine Medical Center. She had suffered severe brain damage and would be hospitalized for a long time. I was working the evening shift at Mercy, so I went every morning to her hospital room and helped her dress, eat, and bathe, and I walked with her around the unit. She had a lot of trouble talking and managing the activities of daily living. She had severe tremors throughout her entire body. Sometimes her whole body would shake and the muscles would tense up, causing incredible pain that couldn't be relieved by medication. I started massaging her, first her hands and arms and then her whole body. It helped enough to allow her to go to sleep. It broke my heart to see her in such shape. She had been such a vibrant woman. The two of us had talked about sailing around the world, which wasn't out of the realm of possibilities because she had been an avid sailor. Now she looked like an old, decrepit lady, and she would never sail anywhere. She ended up at a rehabilitation hospital, where they would help her to regain some, but not all of her skills.

Meanwhile, my job continued to get worse, and I didn't feel like I was making any headway. One evening, a young little nurse sat down with me and proceeded to tell me about all of the mistakes I was making, about hospital rules and nursing laws and what I needed to do to shape up if I wanted to stay there. She then began to tell me that my voice was too loud and that my haircut was too severe, and that if I changed my voice and let my hair grow out, I would do better at communicating with patients. I knew I wasn't doing well, and it felt like it was a real setup for failure. I was so tired and depressed, this new blow just knocked me right over. Try as I might, I couldn't keep myself from crying in front of her. I remember that I kind of dissociated again that night, for the first time in years. I just sat in the nurses' station and stared for a long time. Somehow I finished my work that evening, but I don't know how. I was in a trance. It felt like I was falling—falling from a cliff and there was nothing to land on. I just kept falling. In some ways it was a freeing kind of experience, but I felt like I was getting further and further away from the world. Nothing seemed to matter.

I went home that night, and my old friend, suicide, was waiting for me at the door. There she was, dusted off and waiting for me to reach out and take hold of her once again. I couldn't figure out what to do. I had done all of this recovery work. I had worked myself to the bone going to nursing school, only to find out that I was a terrible nurse. I had ruined a marriage, a relationship, and I had no idea what my sexual identity was. I owed what seemed like a million dollars to the IRS, when you added up penalties and interest, which was compounding daily since I couldn't pay any of it. I also owed a bundle to the state tax people, who hounded me weekly by phone, asking what I was doing to pay them back. Going to school full-time didn't count for anything. So now I was in debt to the tune of about $50,000, and I had nothing to show for it! It seemed like any day I would get fired from my job. I was utterly confused about my sexuality. I was so depressed. I felt like I had fallen down into a deep well, with nothing to grab hold of to pull myself out. I was about to drown. The only thing I had to grab hold of was my old companion, suicide. There she was, waiting for me. And so I decided I would give it considerable thought.

As the next morning dawned, I got up from a horrible night of fitful sleep and terrible dreams, feeling like I had been run over by a car. I called Mercy and told them I was sick and wouldn't be in to work. I sat down and wrote letters to my daughter and to my friends Barbara and Merilyn. I didn't know what else to do. I sat silent in my apartment all day. The phone didn't ring, and no one came to the door. I guess I was waiting for someone or something to stop me, but no one did. This seemed like a relief to finally follow this through. Why had I waited all these years anyway? There was a wet wool blanket of sadness over me as I made sure my two cats had plenty of food and water. I got out a brand-new, single-edge razor blade, wrapped it in paper and stuffed it into my jeans pocket. I took four aspirin. At about 6:00 in the evening, I got into my car and drove to the beach at Kettle Cove in Cape Elizabeth. I walked down to the beach and sat down.

And here I am.

"Most folks are about as happy
as they make up their minds to be."
—Abraham Lincoln

CHAPTER 21

another day has dawned

I opened my eyes to discover I had been sitting there with the video under my eyelids running all night long. It was now daylight—the sun was beginning to rise over the horizon, a big yellow ball in an incredibly orange sky. I looked around and something seemed very different. I felt a presence with me—the same presence I had felt in that camp by the lake, the same one I felt when I was flying in my airplane, the same presence I felt in my little cabin when I quit drinking. It must have been God. There He was, with me the whole time. He never left me. I just hadn't reached out and asked for His help. Once again, I tried to handle things on my own. However, the problems that drove me there the night before somehow didn't seem as big now. My life review helped me to see how far I had come.

I looked around, and although everything looked the same, it felt different than it had the previous night. I began to believe perhaps I was stronger than I had given myself credit for. Suicide was like an addiction that I turned to when the going got tough. I realized I had choices. I always had choices. Wasn't that what I had always taught my clients? I could choose to get through this. I didn't have to kill myself. It wasn't that I was afraid to die—I had done a lot of work around the concept of my own death, and I believed that our spirit and soul go on to another life after we succumb here on earth. I just really didn't want to die right then. I looked around. No one was on the beach, and if I squinted just right, I could still see my little red car in the parking lot a mile away. Nothing had changed. The world had gone to sleep while I was sitting there watching my life video inside my eyelids. It waited for me. But now I felt the presence of God with me, reaching out to take my hand. The sailboat was still over there by Richmond Island, its occupants probably still sleeping, for there was no movement on the boat. Seagulls were flying and squawking, looking for their breakfast, and the sound of fishing boats roared in the distance as they began their day, oblivious to the fact that a woman had almost killed herself on this beautiful beach the night before. The world would continue to turn whether I was there or not.

It was Sunday morning. I had not slept one minute of the night, but I didn't really feel tired. I rubbed tears out of my eyes and looked at myself, realizing I had come too far on my difficult journey to stop now. As I began to get up, I noticed how stiff my body was from sitting against the rocks all night. Good penance, I thought.

As I began the walk back to my car, it seemed like my feet weren't touching the sand, like I was floating or being carried along the beach. The presence of God was still with me, and I felt safe. When I returned to my car, there was, thankfully, no ticket on the windshield. Guess the cops were somewhere else the night before. The thought crossed my mind that maybe I wasn't even there at all—that I really didn't even exist. But I let that idea travel right out of my head. A little crazy thinking. Sounded too much like the old days.

I got home to be greeted by my cats, who rubbed up against me to let me know how much they'd missed me. Everything was just the same as when I left. So what would I do to make things different? How would I cope with everything if I didn't, or couldn't, kill myself? I had no idea.

"And since you cannot see yourself,
so well as by reflection, I, your glass,
will modestly discover to yourself,
that of yourself which you yet
know not of."
—William Shakespeare

CHAPTER 22

terry: twenty-eight days

My financial situation was a huge problem, and my salary as a new nurse didn't begin to take care of things. Maybe I could salvage my job by going to the nurse manager, talking to him about my situation, and asking for more help with training and orientation. I just couldn't imagine getting a second part-time job, but I needed the money. The idea of a roommate didn't appeal to me because the apartment was so small, and who on earth would want to live with me? So I began looking in the classified section of the Sunday paper in the Help Wanted section to see if there was something I could do part-time to earn some extra money. Maybe I could find something different from hospital nursing.

Right there, where it didn't belong, in the jobs section, was an ad, obviously misplaced by the newspaper, by a man looking for a roommate. It said he was a swimmer, that he liked feminine energy, and that he needed to be on the bus line. He wanted to live on Munjoy Hill, which was where I lived. Before I even gave it any thought, I found myself calling this guy. What was I thinking?

The person who answered had a deep, melodious voice. His name was Terry, and he said he had been living out in the country and needed to be in the city because he was working at LL Bean and going to USM to finish up his master's thesis. He said he was temporarily without a car, and so he needed to be on the bus line. I said that I was on the bus line, I lived near the Eastern Promenade, and I had just graduated from USM. I don't know what possessed me to do this—it went against all of my own rules, but I invited him over so I could meet him. He said he could come that day. I knew nothing about him. And I didn't even want a roommate—I wanted a part-time job! What if he was an ax murderer? If I had a roommate, wouldn't it make more sense to have a woman, since I only had one bathroom? I didn't even know what I would charge for rent, and I wasn't even sure if the landlord would be agreeable to my having a roommate since my lease said I would be living there alone. What was I thinking? But I felt this compelling urge to do it anyway. The presence of God was still very strong, and it felt so right. I sure didn't understand, but I went with it.

When he showed up, I can't begin to describe the feelings that surged through me when I answered the door. There stood a handsome, six-foot, four-inch man, who looked to be the same age as me, with a canvas book bag slung over his shoulder. I immediately felt an incredible spiritual connection to this man, even before he walked into the apartment. I had never felt anything like it, except for the times when I had felt the presence of God, like this morning on the beach, only the feelings were a direct link to him—almost between our bellies. The feeling didn't subside. I showed him the apartment, apologizing for its size. He just nodded and grunted as he looked into each room, sizing it up in his head. Then I made some iced tea and we went out onto the back deck to sit and talk. He was so tall he hit his head on the rafters, which I had never even noticed were there! I thought he was rather charming and he had incredibly deep eyes. What was happening to me? In order to keep him from ever thinking we would have a romantic relationship, I told him I was a lesbian. He looked at me, and after a few moments of silence, a smile broke out on his face, and he said, "I doubt that very much." I was furious! How could he judge me like that? I said as much. He said, "Well, if you're a lesbian, I guess that's okay with me. I don't usually like women who are lesbians, though." What a bigot! I wasn't going to let someone like this live with me! Then one of my cats jumped onto his lap, purring and offering and requesting affection. Terry looked at me and said, "I don't like cats, either." So

I reached over and removed the cat from his lap, who immediately jumped back onto his lap! He didn't push the cat off, and in fact he began to pet the cat affectionately! What was this guy, some kind of comedian?

He shared with me that he had epilepsy, but he hadn't had a seizure in a long time. Even still, he had lost his driver's license due to a seizure a few months back and he needed to be on the bus line until he cleared things up and got his license renewed. He assured me that the seizures were under control because he was on a new drug called Neurontin. (I would surely look that up in my nurse's drug book after he left!) He said he didn't drink and didn't smoke. Those were plusses. We continued to talk, and I found talking to him to be very comfortable, even with his confrontational style. The longer we talked, the stronger that spiritual connection grew. And his laughter was intoxicating! He would laugh from deep in his belly, with sort of a "heh, heh, heh," like James Earl Jones. I finally asked him if he felt anything weird going on between us. He said he did—that he'd felt it the minute he walked into the apartment. Wow! What the heck was going on?

After about an hour of conversation, he said, "Well, what do you think? Do you want me for a roommate?"

My answer was a question: "Do you want to be my roommate? Isn't this place too small for you? You don't like cats, and you don't like lesbians! You're too tall to walk around without hitting your head. Why would you want to live here?"

He was silent for a minute or two, and then he said, "I like your energy. I like it here. It feels right. How soon can I move in?" He didn't even ask how much the rent was. He liked my energy? He had no idea that I had just last night come very close to committing suicide! But then, hadn't that brought me closer to God?

I finally said, "Okay, I guess we can give it a try. When do you want to move in?"

"How about tomorrow?"

I said, "No, that's really too soon. I have some things I have to do to make your room ready for you. How about Wednesday or

Thursday?"

We settled on Wednesday. He asked about the rent and I said, "How much can you afford?"

He said about $275.

I said, "Then the rent will be $275, heat and utilities included. You buy your own groceries."

It was settled. He gave me some money to seal the deal. He called a friend to give him a ride to work and left.

Holy shit! What on earth had I just done? Was I nuts? In the span of twenty-four hours I had gone from being suicidal to having a man move into my house! What was going on? I felt like I was on some kind of roller-coaster ride, and I had to just hang on!

I wasn't scheduled to work that day, so I used the time to do some house cleaning and get the spare bedroom emptied out. I had no idea what I was doing. I felt as if I was now running on some kind of autopilot that I had to just trust. I felt like I was in God's arms and He would take care of me. But it sure seemed strange. I went to bed that night, and for the first time in a long time, I prayed—for guidance and wisdom. I slept deeply, and had a dream of a snake. When I woke up, my memory of the snake made me think of new life. Was I starting a new life? After breakfast, I went out for a bike ride along the shore and decided I was going to have to make a fresh start at work somehow. The fresh ocean air exhilarated me, and I felt a new surge of energy coming into my life.

It is incredible to me how the human species can be so resilient. Over and over again, I have been in harm's way and have somehow been rescued, and I have found a way to bounce back. I don't believe that we live in a vacuum. I believe that our whole universe is intentional, and that we're all here for a reason. I might never figure out what the reason is, but I know that all of this isn't just a coincidence. And maybe for the first time, I was feeling like I actually belonged here.

I guess everyone ponders the question of life—why we live, what we're here for. I certainly have asked those questions over and over and have never gotten an answer. But somehow, that morning, I was beginning to feel an answer forming in my mind. Did it have anything to do with Terry? How could it? Why wouldn't it? Did it have something to do with the fact that I had almost killed myself for the third time? The last time I tried to do that, I saw a bright light and quit drinking. This time, I got Terry! Hmmmmmm.

I went to work early that afternoon and headed to the hospital's medical library to put in a request for literature on epilepsy. Then I went and requested a meeting with the nurse manager, Joe. When we sat down to talk, I told him that I was aware I hadn't been doing a very good job, and that I wanted to start over. I confessed that coming out of USM I hadn't felt adequately prepared for the level of nursing I was working in, and I probably should have accepted a job at a nursing home where the pace was slower and I would have had the chance to develop my skills and learn how to be a nurse. But, now, here I was. I asked him if he wanted me to quit. He said no, that I wasn't as bad as I was making myself out to be. He agreed to pair me up with a nurse whom I felt comfortable with (obviously, not the one who had accosted me the other night!), and she would mentor me for a few weeks. This sounded good and it offered me a fresh start.

That night, while working, the nurse who had confronted me came up to me and said, "I noticed that you're talking softer. You must have listened to me the other night. Doesn't it feel better to be talking softer?" To be honest, I wanted to hit her, but I had never hit anyone, and I wouldn't start now. I just glared at her. She was like Nurse Ratchet in the movie *One Flew over the Cuckoo's Nest.* And I felt like the patient who had just been thrown into the psychiatric ward by accident!

The next day, I decided to get my guitar out, dust it off, and start playing and singing again. It had been awhile since I'd had any music in my life. I got out a songbook and looked for something new to learn.. It felt good to be playing my guitar and singing again.

On Wednesday, July 28, 1997, Terry moved in with me. I left the door unlocked for him because I wouldn't be home when he came with his furniture. How trusting was that? When I got home, he was all moved in and sitting at his computer like he had been there for years. He said hello without looking up, and I just smiled to myself. Why did this feel so comfortable? Who was this man? I just scratched my head and walked away. I went about my usual routine, which included doing some yoga and taking a hot bath before going to bed. I thought I should lock the bathroom door when I went in for my bath, but somehow it didn't seem like I needed to. I lay there in the tub full of bubbles, knowing that Terry was in the other room—this complete stranger who had walked into my life—and it felt like he belonged there. It was almost as though we were an old married couple! This had gone against all of my rules about getting to know people—especially men. But even though I felt in my gut it was right, I didn't understand any of it.

Each day with Terry brought something new. He was an interesting character. His communication style was more direct than mine. And he was louder. And very opinionated. He started the first day by making up an elaborate work schedule, which he put on the refrigerator. It had room on it for my schedule. He wanted each of us to be aware of each other's work schedules. As it turned out, our schedules were the same on most days. I worked the evening shift four days a week, with my off days varying each week. He worked mostly evenings at LL Bean on the telephones taking catalog orders. Terry was an incredibly bright man, but because of his lifelong epilepsy, he could never hold down a full-time professional job. Who wants to be in a meeting led by a man who has seizures? So he was working a temporary, part-time menial job taking calls from catalog shoppers. At least he had the right voice for it. His voice was deep and clear, and you could say, rather sexy. I learned that he had done a lot of radio work earlier in his life. He said he had previously worked at USM Nursing School as a janitor, while taking his last couple of master's courses there. My ears perked up—had I ever seen him on campus? I couldn't remember. What a coincidence!

So with our schedules posted, he then wanted to know whether I wanted to have meals together. This had happened so suddenly that I hadn't given it any thought. I had never had a roommate before, so I didn't know what the protocol was.

We had breakfast together, after which he washed the dishes, talking and laughing the whole time. I went for a bike ride and got ready for work. Since Terry was scheduled to go to work a half hour before me, I offered to give him a ride. He clearly stated to me that he wasn't expecting rides from me, that he could take the bus. He had the schedule and knew where it picked up passengers. I said, "Okay, but I'll still offer the ride if you want it." He took the ride. Since he had lived in the Portland area for more than twenty-five years, he knew shortcuts I had never heard of. So it was dashing through back alleys and little unnamed streets that I gave him a ride to work that first day. I didn't try to return by way of the shortcuts—I surely would have gotten lost. One thing I never had was a sense of direction. I could follow a map very well, but if someone said turn north onto Route whatever, I wouldn't know which way to turn. And if I lose sight of the main streets, I get hopelessly confused. I had hoped this would clear up when I got sober, but it didn't. Guess God has a sense of humor!

Terry and I had also agreed, out of mutual courtesy, to inform the other when we expected to be home, and to call and leave a message if we would be late. I thought this made sense. When I got home from work, Terry was sitting up in his bed, reading. I stuck my head around the corner and said hello to him. He ignored me and didn't even look up. I decided I wouldn't take it personally. Guess we all have a right to our privacy. This apartment was so small that it would take an effort for each of us to honor each other's space. I was still scratching my head, wondering why I had done this!

In the meantime, my job began to progress a little better. Nurse Ratchett was now working the day shift, and I had been assigned to a seasoned, gentle nurse to mentor me. I had developed a better attitude, and there was hope for the future.

My visits to Merilyn at Maine Medical Center continued until one day when she was transferred to New England Rehabilitation Hospital. I took her over there and helped her to get admitted. She still couldn't remember much of anything, and she couldn't even sign her own name. I made regular visits to her, even attending some of her occupational therapy groups with her, in an effort to learn what she was learning and what she still needed to do for rehab. She was seriously depressed, and it was impossible to get her to smile. I also helped with her activities of daily living. One day, I was helping her to take a shower in a big, walk-in shower designed for people in wheelchairs or on crutches. As I was helping her dry herself off, she lost her balance and started to fall backward. I caught her just in time, and she said, "Gee, I almost went sailing!" I responded with, "Well, isn't that what you want to do—go sailing?" A smile broke out on her face and she began to laugh uncontrollably. It broke the ice, and her depression started to lift. Her boyfriend, Gregg, came in the evenings after he got off work. I attended a family case conference with the treatment team, Merilyn, and Gregg, and they said that she wasn't progressing as fast as they had hoped. They didn't know for sure what parts of her brain had been damaged or how to treat it, since it was something with which they had very little experience. This was a blow, and very sad to hear. Merilyn had never gotten a nursing job, and now she never would. In fact, she likely would never be able to do any kind of paid employment again. For someone as bright and vibrant as she was, it was very depressing to learn this news. I realized it was a loss in my life as well. She had become such an important friend to me. Now, she wasn't the same person. I loved her, though, and I wouldn't abandon her.

The second night with Terry, something strange happened that I wouldn't learn the truth about until much later. He was, again, sitting up in bed reading when I got home, and, again, I stuck my head in and said hello, to which he did not respond. About ten minutes later, as I was walking through the hallway, he got up, in his nightshirt, walked into the hallway, and walked right into me, as though I wasn't there. He didn't say anything, and I just kind of stepped out of the way. I thought it was strange, and I tried to talk to him, but he headed for the bathroom, closed the door, and ignored me. Another ten minutes went by, and he came into the kitchen where I was making a cup of tea. He looked at me with surprise and said, "I didn't know you were home." I just looked at him, dumbfounded. Was he playing tricks on me? What was going on? But before I could address this question, he sat down, asked if I would make him a cup of tea also, and proceeded to talk. He talked nonstop about so many things, I can't remember where one subject left off and another began. He talked about his childhood, when the epilepsy had first been diagnosed, at age four. He talked about his family, and how he felt like the black sheep of the family because of his epilepsy and his failure to be a high achiever like his siblings. His sister was a physician's assistant in New York, one brother was a lawyer in a very large firm, working in Paris, France, and his other brother was a very successful banker in Houston, Texas. Terry felt like a failure, and he felt that his family looked down on him. I could relate to that, I told him.

We talked into the wee hours of the morning, mostly about Terry's past. He told me that his father had committed suicide at age fifty-two when Terry was twenty-one years old. He spoke with such anger and venom that it became obvious he had not done all of his grief work and he hadn't let go of any of his anger. He said that committing suicide is the ultimate "fuck you" to the people left behind. I silently thought about the fact that less than a week ago, I had almost committed suicide. What would he think of me if he knew? What would that "fuck you" mean to my daughter and my few friends if I had carried it through? Finally, with much protest from Terry, I closed my door and went to bed.

The next morning, I got up, went for a brisk bike ride, and then went to the music store to buy a couple of new CDs to play on my stereo. They were both piano music, sort of easy listening kind of stuff that soothed my soul. I wanted to start writing in a journal and I needed the right background music to tune out the rest of the world. When I came home, Terry wanted to know where I had gone. I was a little incensed; he didn't need to know my every whereabouts and every move. But I didn't want to argue with him so I simply told him where I had gone and showed him my CDs. He wanted to hear them, so we sat on the couch and I put them in the CD player. (This little tickling I kept feeling in my brain made me think that someone had sent this character into my life to keep an eye on me!)

We sat on the couch drinking tea as Terry talked more about his childhood and important people in his life. He talked about a family from Pennsylvania that became a pseudo family for him—people who were more like family to him than his own. Their name was Wheeler. My heart skipped a beat. What a coincidence! I said that I had a pseudo family named Wheeler also when I was a child. He just smiled and kept talking. (My Wheeler family had relatives in Pennsylvania—I wondered if they were the same family!)

He kept talking as though he hadn't heard me say anything. He started telling me about when he was first diagnosed with epilepsy. He described the time at four or five years old when he had his first seizure—or, that is, the first seizure that anyone noticed. What he could remember of it was feeling like he had fallen asleep, or drifted off, and when he woke up, his sister, Liza, was all upset and had gone to get their mother. He said that after that he was taken to doctors and eventually put on medication that doped him up. He said it kept him from concentrating or being able to pay attention at school, the consequences of which kept him in the teacher's punitive eye. The seizures, as well as the anti-seizure medication, kept him from ever realizing his real potential academically and socially, and because of this, he felt like he was the black sheep of the family. He said his father was afraid that he would have a seizure when they had company, so they would parade him out to meet the guests and then banish him to his room for the remainder of the evening. He felt like the family pet. This was probably why he felt closer to the Wheelers than his own family. He didn't feel judged by them as he did by his own family. (I don't believe that his family would remember these situations in the same way.) His childhood was filled with doctor visits and trial medications, all of which either made him feel doped up or didn't prevent the seizures.

As I sat there and watched him talk, he seemed as though he was transfixed somewhere else, like he was in a dissociative state. And I felt a pang of empathy, maybe even sympathy for him. I also felt a kindred spirit with him. We both believed we were damaged goods. It seemed we had quite a bit in common after all. But why was this handsome, six-foot-four man sitting in my living room? Why was he living with me? It confounded me!

I had to go to work, and I got ready and left at about 2:30. Terry was working later that day and would find his own way to his job. At work, I decided to really try harder to concentrate on being a good nurse and try to tune everything else out of my mind. As I admitted to my coworkers that I hadn't done a very good job up to this point, they were empathetic and seemed ready to give me another chance. One nurse said that when I first started, she had decided I would never make it, but now, she had hope for me! This was a lift to my spirits. But I knew I wasn't out of the woods yet. I realized that I hadn't asked enough questions, that I would pretend I knew something when I didn't. That type of behavior most likely came from my childhood, where it wasn't safe to ask questions or there was no one to ask. I thought I had gotten rid of that stuff! Damn! Was it ever going to go away?

When I got home from work at midnight, Terry was up making a cup of tea and asked if I wanted to walk down to the shore and walk along the trail with him. I loved to walk on the shore at night, but I didn't always feel safe alone. "Yes," I told him, "I would love to. Let's go!" As we walked on the shore, I was taken in by the stars, the fragrance of the ocean, and the ambiance of the night. I wanted to walk in silence and just soak it all in. But it wouldn't be so. Terry wanted or needed to talk. And talk, he did. I confess, I was a little irritated that he wouldn't just shut up and enjoy the silence and listen to the distant sounds of the harbor. He talked about how all of the homes and business in Portland had once dumped all of their waste water into the ocean. There used to be huge pipes that ran into the water. All of the sewage of the entire city went into the ocean. He said that about twenty years ago, he and some other people had formed an organization called Friends of Casco Bay, a nonprofit, volunteer-run organization that would try to address the pollution problems in the Casco Bay before all of the fish were gone. By his account, he had been an incredibly loud political activist. I would suspect, by what he was saying, he didn't automatically make a lot of friends. He continued to tell me about how the city eventually built collecting tubes and started a waste-water treatment plant, which was right there at the shore, and that now the water in the bay was beginning to be cleaned up. I asked why he was no longer active in these endeavors, and he said he was just worn out and had made too many enemies. At some point, we stopped walking and just stood, silently (finally), and looked out at the ocean. After a few minutes, I realized it was getting late, and I said I wanted to walk back toward home. Terry just stood there, ignoring me, and continued to stare out at the ocean. Why was this man so arrogant? I began walking away, and he didn't join me, so I just walked home alone. Eventually he came home, and never said a word about why he had just stood there the way he had. I thought he was just being rude.

I was still volunteering for the Maine Lesbian Gay Political Activists, and the next day I went down to their office to help stuff envelopes for an upcoming vote by the citizens in Maine on whether or not gays should share equal rights with everyone else. My questioning if I was truly a lesbian didn't change my strong feelings on this issue, and I wanted to help this cause in any way I could. As I sat there stuffing envelopes and talking with everyone, I began to notice that I didn't feel like I fit in anymore. Actually, I never felt like I fit in there; I had just been trying to find a place in the world that worked for me. I didn't think this would be it. Did Terry's presence in my life have something to do with this? I was more confused than ever.

About noon that day, Terry asked if I would like to go to the beach with him. It was a bright, hot, sunny day—good beach weather. I said yes, enthusiastically. Off we went to Kettle Cove. I was not about to tell Terry that I had been there three weeks ago and spent the night on the rocks. Once we found a place to settle on the beach, I put my umbrella in the sand and set up my beach chair, then got out my cold drink and a book to read. Terry announced that he was going to get undressed and change into his bathing suit. He meant right there on the beach! I shouted my disapproval of this.

"What are you talking about? You can't just strip down to nothing here on the beach! Why didn't you put your trunks on under your clothes? There is a bathroom back by the parking lot, why don't you go use that?"

He was incensed that I would suggest such a thing, and he compromised by changing his clothes behind a bush! What was wrong with this guy? Scratching my head, I wondered what in God's name I had gotten myself into. And why! He said he was going to go swimming and asked if I wanted to go with him. I said no, because I wasn't really much of a swimmer. I go in the water and get wet and splash around, and then sit under my umbrella and let the breeze dry me off. So Terry walked down the beach and then out into the water, stopping at about waist deep. I expected to see him dive in and swim, but instead, he just stood there with his hands stretched out to his sides, sort of moving them in a rhythmic circular motion. He stood there for a long time. Eventually he walked back to the blanket and didn't go swimming. When he came back, I asked him why he didn't go swimming. He answered, "What do you mean? I did go swimming!" My head was spinning. I know he did not go swimming. He'd just stood there. It was then that the reality of his situation began to penetrate my denial. All of these odd behaviors of his, this one included, were about him having seizures. He had mentioned when I first met him that he didn't have grand mal seizures, but temporal lobe seizures. With temporal lobe seizures, a person is in sort of a blackout, and they continue to appear somewhat functional, but they really aren't functioning and they are not conscious. This explained why Terry acted strangely sometimes, didn't know when I was around, and denied doing things I had clearly seen him doing. When I thought about it, these seizures were happening at least once per day, maybe more! And he wasn't aware that they were happening. He was taking 3,000 milligrams of Neurontin, a new anti-seizure drug. My nursing drug manual told me that this was just about the top end of the recommended dosage. He couldn't take any more than this, and it wasn't working.

On our way home from the beach, I decided to talk to Terry about this. "You had a seizure on the beach today, Terry. I saw you," I said. He looked at me with anger and fear in his eyes and denied it. I mentioned the other times at the apartment when I suspected he was having seizures as well, and again he denied them. I said that I suspected he was having more seizures than he was aware of. Again, he denied it. So I dropped the subject. We were completely silent all the way home, and he didn't talk to me the rest of the day.

The next day, we were sitting in the kitchen talking at breakfast, and he began to act strange. His head began this back-and-forth movement for no apparent reason, and his eyes were kind of glazed over, like a deer stuck in the headlights. His hands began an awkward movement, almost like swimming. I reached over and touched his arm and said his name. He stopped and blinked and looked around and then said "hi," like he had just walked into the room. The whole episode didn't last more than two minutes. But he was disoriented afterward. When I thought he was all the way back with me, I told him, "Terry, you just had a seizure. I watched you." He looked at me and I thought I saw tears well up in his eyes. He looked away and said, "Well, maybe I am having some minor seizures. I'll tell my doctor about it when I go to see him next week, and maybe he can increase my dose of Neurontin." I told him that it didn't scare me (that was a lie), and that it wouldn't affect our roommate relationship. However, I wanted to know what I could do to help him. He said that doing just what I did, to touch him and say his name, would help him to come back to reality, and that it would be good to know whenever he had one. I said I would do that. He then began talking about the legal battle he was having trying to get his license back, and I was aghast! I said, "Terry, you shouldn't drive. You're having these seizures every day, and there doesn't seem to be anything in particular that triggers them, which means you can't control them. I'm sorry to say, but I would not ride in a car with you if you were driving." He was not happy about this, and said so, then he said he was going to continue his fight to get his freedom and his human rights restored. (Driving is a privilege, not a right.)

I looked at this tall, handsome, intelligent, wonderful man and realized that he felt like a caged animal. Because of his seizure disorder, he was losing many of the rights and opportunities that all of us take for granted. It broke my heart. I wanted to reach out and just hug him, but I didn't. I also began to realize that he was depressed. I mean, he was in a serious depression. He tried hard to conceal it with his laughter and the fact that he went to work every day and went to the YWCA four times a week swimming. It was kind of like how I concealed my own depression. But I could see that he was depressed. I recognized depression—I should. I had experienced it enough in my life! He had been here a total of ten days, and already so much had unfolded. I was again questioning why he was here and what this was all about. I felt like I was on some kind of weird magic carpet ride, and I wasn't sure who was driving!

I continued my visits to Merilyn, and she seemed to be progressing, very slowly, toward some rehabilitation. But it was clear that she would never regain all of the abilities and skills she had once had. I told her about Terry, and she got a twinkle in her eye, the first time I had seen this since her accident, and said, "Oh, are you getting smitten with him?"

"No!" I said. "Remember, I'm a lesbian."

She laughed and said, "I never really believed you were a lesbian, and now I'm sure of it." God, she knew me! What a wonderful friend she was. I loved this woman, and it just killed me to see her sitting there shaking and not able to eat on her own. I always cried when I left her.

Terry asked me if I would go to the YWCA with him and be a spotter while he swam. Swimming was the only type of exercise he felt comfortable doing, since he had trouble with his knees. Many pools had banned him because of his seizure disorder, and so, concerned about liability issues, the YWCA required a spotter, someone to watch him while he swam. Terry had an elaborate schedule of swimming dates and names of people who could spot for him. He would spend at least an hour every morning on the phone trying to line people up to spot for him and give him rides. He kept a daily list of things he had to do, and as he accomplished each thing, he would cross it out. It was a 5 x 8 piece of paper that he would fold and put into his shirt pocket and carry with him all day. If he didn't accomplish something on the list, it went on the next day's list. I was impressed with such organization, but then I realized that he had to do this; because of his seizures he would forget where he was or whether he had done something or been somewhere. So, anyway, I agreed to spot for him a couple times per week as my schedule would permit. Watching him swim, I could see how he escaped from his painful world for at least a half an hour each day and felt renewed afterward.

One day, when I wasn't working, he called me at about 5:00

and said he was at USM doing some work on his master's thesis. He wanted to know if we could eat dinner together. I said yes and offered to pick him up. He said he would walk. I thought it was kind of a hike, but with his long legs, he could make it in about twenty minutes. He said he would be home no later than 6:00. So I was kind of excited and began cooking dinner. Six o'clock came and went, and no Terry. At 7:30 he came walking in the back door, and I had already eaten. He looked at me, and there was blood running down the side of his face. I asked him what had happened to him, and he didn't know what I was talking about. He was upset because I hadn't waited dinner for him. I said, "Look at the clock. It's 7:30!"

He answered, "It is not. I walked straight from USM to here without stopping. It can't be 7:30." But as he looked at the clock, he realized he was wrong. I asked why he had blood on his face, and he said he didn't have blood on his face.

I reached up and drew a drop of it off onto my finger and showed him. He went and looked into the mirror, and had no idea how he banged his head.

I said, "I wonder if you had a seizure on your way home and fell down."

He closed his eyes and said, "You know, I seem to remember walking through the same intersection more than once, now that I think about it. Maybe you're right."

I bet he walked the route from USM to Munjoy Hill a couple of times and tripped and fell down, all in a seizure-induced blackout. How did he keep from getting hit by a car? He would have had to walk through rush hour traffic, right across the Franklin Arterial, where cars drive fast and furious on their way home from work. He must have had an angel on his shoulder! So, taking pity on him, I got out the leftovers and warmed up some dinner for him.

Every chance he got, Terry continued to talk about his family and his childhood. His Quaker religion was very important to him, but he said he currently was not attending meetings at the meeting house. I asked why, and he said, "Because I got into a disagreement with someone there who said I threatened her, and the elders of the church had a meeting and decided I needed to stay away for a while. I think it's probably okay for me to go back now, because the woman who complained about me is gone."

I asked if I could go with him sometime, because I was searching for some foundation for my own spiritual growth and had never found a church that fit for me. And I remembered my stay at the Rufus Jones House in China when I first moved to Maine, reading the diaries and journals there. He said that maybe I could go with him; he would think about it. He seemed hurt by the elders' decision to keep him away. He clearly believed he had not done anything wrong. And he was a "birthright" Quaker. He had been going there his whole life.

I felt compassion and empathy for Terry. Even though our stories weren't the same, we shared some of life's miseries. For both of us, no matter how hard we tried, life seemed to give us additional challenges every step of the way. We felt abandoned, rejected, and outcast. And both of us were "underachievers" relative to our abilities. Why was this man in my life? I had no clue.

I went to visit Barbara one sunny, August day. We had lunch and sat by the Kennebec River to talk. I told her about Terry. She finally said to me, "I think you are falling in love with this man." I was infuriated! "No, I'm not," I shouted. "I—he—you don't understand. I can't be in love with him. I barely know him. I'm just trying to figure out why he's in my life."

She answered, "I think you're being prepared for something."

I was silent. A thought something like that had crossed my mind also, but I hadn't verbalized it. What was I being prepared for? She suggested that I keep following my gut instincts. I trusted Barbara's advice. She had been my surrogate mother from the day I met her, and a wonderful, lifelong friend. I wouldn't have talked to her if I wasn't prepared to hear her answers.

So I went back home and tried to stop my silent questioning of everything that occurred. I tried to just go with the flow.

One night when I arrived home from work at around 1:00 a.m., I stuck my head in Terry's room and he greeted me, but he was not smiling. He asked me to come into his room and sit on his bed. I did. He then asked me if I would hold him. It wasn't a sexual gesture. It was more like a child asking his mother for comfort. I lay down on his bed and held him, as best I could, in my arms. We stayed that way for at least a couple of hours, and when he was asleep, I tiptoed out and went into my own bedroom. I couldn't sleep. I lay there thinking of Terry. Why did he need me to hold him? It made tears come to my eyes.

The next day was a routine day for me. On my way home from work, I noticed the full moon just peeking over the horizon on the ocean. I ran into the apartment and excitedly told Terry, "You have to go outside and see this moon. It's spectacular!" His eyes lit up, he jumped up and put his clothes on, and we walked outside and down to the shore and looked at the moon as it was rising in the night sky. I can't describe how it felt. It seemed like there was nothing else in the world at that moment except what I could see around me. It was perfect.

When we got back to the apartment, we discovered that the only way we could see the moon from the window was to lie on the floor. So, we both lay down on the living room floor and stared at the moon. I had put my new CDs on the stereo to listen to, and it was just a magical moment in time.

Later that week, Terry said that the YWCA would be closing for two weeks for an overhaul of the pool and he would have to find another place to swim. He said he would call his friend, Marlee Turner, who owned a place called Northern Pines Resort in Raymond, on Crescent Lake. She was a Quaker and had been his friend for twenty years. She would let him swim there. But he had no transportation. So I agreed on my day off to take him out to swim. On Sunday, we made the one-hour trip out to Northern Pines to go swimming. There were a couple of floating docks connected to the shore for people to sit on or dive off from, as well as a floating platform a little farther out. Terry said he would swim back and forth between the dock and the platform, and we began shedding our clothes and unfolding our beach chairs. I was sitting in my beach chair watching Terry as he got his swim goggles and all his swim paraphernalia ready. As he bent over to pick something up, he went into a seizure. His arms began moving in a swimming motion and his head went back and forth, like the breathing movement of a swimmer, but in kind of a jerky fashion. The floating dock began bobbing up and down, and I was afraid he would fall backward into the water, so I grabbed his arm and wrestled him into the beach chair. Other people, guests of the Northern Pines Resort, were watching, and I told them it was okay and not to worry. I stroked Terry's arm and gently called his name, and after a few minutes, he seemed to come out of it. I was shaking like a leaf! He looked at me and said "hi."

I said, "You just had a seizure."

He looked around and noticed people's stares and said, "Oh."

I said, "You should rest a few minutes before going swimming. From what I've read about seizures, it takes a lot of energy out of your body. Why don't we just sit here for fifteen minutes or so till you regain some energy? Have something to drink."

He wasn't having any part of it. "I know what's best for me, I can swim just fine. I'm not tired." And with that, he jumped in the water and began swimming toward the floating platform.

Remember, I'm not much of a swimmer, and I'm even a little afraid of the water, especially when I can't see the bottom. But I jumped in right behind him and tried like hell to keep up with him, to no avail. He was meeting me on his return lap and I tried to turn and stay with him, but again, he turned and met me again on the next lap. I got tired quickly and gave up and went back to my chair. That was enough for me! What was I thinking anyway? I couldn't rescue this six-foot-four man if I tried. I could barely keep myself afloat! But I would certainly keep an eye on him. He swam for about twenty-five minutes nonstop and then came back and sat down and we had lunch. He seemed fine. He said that the sun's reflection on the water can trigger a seizure, and that's probably what had happened. I began to feel a deeper connection to this man for some reason.

On our way home, I told him that when he had the seizure, I was afraid that he would fall backward in the water and drown. I said, "I am growing quite fond of you, Terry, and I don't want to lose you." With that, he reached over and held my hand and said nothing. I looked at him and thought I saw tears in his eyes. It was a silent ride home, with him holding my hand until I had to shift gears. Was Barbara right? Was I falling in love with him? Nah. This was different from anything like falling in love I had ever experienced. This was much deeper, more spiritual. There seemed to be some underlying purpose, the revelation of which I had not yet seen.

When we got home, there was a message on the answering machine for Terry, from his brother John who was vacationing in Nantucket. Terry called him back and they had a nice talk. I left the apartment so he could have some privacy. When I got back, he said, "Where'd you go? While I had my brother Johnny on the phone, I wanted to ask you if you would be willing to drive me to Nantucket to see my family the weekend after next. I'll pay all the expenses, and you can stay there with us. What do you think?"

I looked at my work schedule. I had a three-day weekend off. I quickly agreed to go with him. I'd never been to Nantucket and thought it would be a great trip. He called his brother back and made the arrangements. I guess John had to make a reservation for the ferry and everything had to be orchestrated "just so" in order to get there. So it was all set. He said his mother was there and his sister, Liza, might be there and possibly his brother Ross from Texas. He was excited to have me meet his family. I was a little confused after having listened to him say how he felt like the black sheep of the family but I didn't say anything. I guess not everyone was estranged from their family like I was. Maybe his was a healthier family than mine.

Later in the day, Terry called his friend Bobbi in Augusta. He asked me if I could drive him up to visit her sometime, when I was planning a visit to my daughter or someone else in Augusta. I said, "Sure, I'd love to." Bobbi was blind, and she had been a friend of Terry's for more than twenty years. Since he had lost his right to drive, he hadn't been able to see her. This seemed to mean a lot to him. We tentatively set the date for that coming weekend. I had to work the night shift that night, so I went to bed and tried to get some sleep prior to going in at 11:00. I hated working nights. It messed up my whole sleep cycle and ruined my days off because I was so tired. But everyone had to take their turn doing nights. When I got home the next morning, I closed my bedroom door, put plugs in my ears and went to sleep. When I got up, Terry was gone to work or school. He came home later that evening and we went down to the ocean trail and walked in the moonlight. There was something in the air, I couldn't pin it down. But something was different. He held my hand as we walked, and I wanted these moments to last forever. We watched the *Scotia Prince* leave on its nightly journey to Nova Scotia and then walked home.

When we got home, we made love. I have no answers for this one. It was a huge surprise to me. But it seemed right. He was kind and gentle and loving. Afterward, Terry chuckled and said, "See, I knew you weren't a lesbian." And I realized that, for the first time ever, I wasn't repulsed by a penis. In fact, I hadn't even thought about it until it was over. How could this be? Maybe this man was helping me to heal, finally, from my lifetime of injuries. He seemed quite satisfied and we slept together in my bed. During the night, I was awakened by his elbow hitting my ribs, and I turned over and realized that he was having a seizure. This poor man. He had been tormented his whole life, even in his sleeping hours. Was there no relief for him? What was the purpose of him being in my life, or me in his? There were so many questions without answers. I found myself thinking about our trip to Nantucket in a couple of weeks, and I decided to buy a new bathing suit.

The next day brought clear skies and sunshine. We had breakfast out on the deck and Terry somehow began thinking of his father. He became angry and pounded his fist on the table and said, "You know, my father committed suicide at age –fifty-two, the same age I am right now. I think that suicide is the ultimate 'fuck you.' Don't you?"

I felt my own face turn red because of my own lifelong obsession with suicide. Seeing how angry it made him, I didn't share it with him.

He seemed to get over his anger quickly. After breakfast, he said he had some banking business to take care of and said he was then going to go out to Northern Pines to swim. I asked him how he was getting there, and he said a friend of Marlee's, someone he hadn't met, was going to give him a ride. At about 2:00, on my way to work, I dropped him off at the bank and watched him walk down the street with his duffel bag over his shoulder, looking like a lost soul. I watched until he disappeared into the bank, and then I went to work, looking forward to seeing him again that night.

That night at work, I took care of a lovely woman in her seventies who had had a mastectomy. This was the specialty of our unit, and I loved taking care of these women. Her husband was in to visit her for a couple of hours. He spent a good deal of his time out at the nurses' station talking to me. He was quite an eccentric character, and it turned out he was a retired professor and a recovering alcoholic. He was an interesting person, but he just wouldn't stop talking. So my biggest challenge that evening was to keep him at bay without hurting his feelings. I think he was there until 10:00, when I encouraged him to go home and get some sleep.

CHAPTER 23

three raccoons

When my shift ended, I went home. I expected to find Terry there, since his work schedule said he worked until 10:00 p.m. But, he wasn't there, and there was no message from him on the machine. He was always very good about this, and I began to wonder if he was okay. At midnight I went to bed, but I found it hard to sleep. In the summertime, there were huge raccoons in the neighborhood, and if you left garbage out, they would find it. The upstairs tenants always left garbage on their deck, and that night, the raccoons were up and down the steps many times, triggering the motion-sensitive lights on the deck. The lights kept waking me up, and I would get up to see if it was Terry coming home. But it never was—only the pesky raccoons. At about 2:00 a.m. I was scared and I decided to call where he worked (LL Bean is open 24/7, 365 days a year), and learned that he didn't go in at all, and didn't call, which they said was highly unusual for him. I remembered the day he came home with a cut on his head and couldn't account for it, and I thought he might have had a seizure and fallen and was hurt somewhere. So I called all of the emergency rooms and the police department. No one had seen him. Now I didn't know what to do, and I couldn't sleep at all. I thought about calling Marlee Turner, thinking that maybe he just decided to stay over in one of her camps for the night. But he would have called me if he had done that. Also, I realized I didn't have her phone number. So I tried to go to bed again, but I tossed and turned. All through the night the raccoons continued to make the lights blink on and off.

"Death may be the greatest
of all human blessings."
—Socrates

CHAPTER 24

three loons

At 4:00 a.m., the phone rang. It was Marlee Turner. I felt my heart go thud when she said that Terry was "missing." She said that he had come out yesterday evening to go swimming and he had assured her that he didn't need anyone to watch him, that he would be okay. He left his duffel bag on the beach with his clothes carefully folded on top. She remembered seeing him swimming his laps for quite a long time, and then he stopped. She expected to see him come up to her house, but he never showed up. The person who was to give him a ride home asked where he was, and they started looking for him, to no avail. They discovered his clothes, untouched, on the shore, and thought the worst—that he had drowned. They looked through the camp and the woods, calling his name, and finally, they called the Cumberland County Sheriff. When the Sheriff's Department arrived, they surrounded the whole complex, barricaded the driveway, and refused to let Marlee use the telephone to call anyone. I guess this was protocol until they ruled out foul play. They brought in dogs that followed Terry's scent to the shore, and then there was nothing. By 4:00 a.m. they had ruled out foul play and said she could call anyone she needed to. The sheriff called the state game warden's diving team to come to the lake to search for his body. They would arrive at dawn. I told Marlee I would get in my car and go out there immediately. With that, I got dressed and called Barbara, waking her up. I told her what had happened and asked for her prayers. I thought I could hear her crying at the other end of the phone, but I said I had to go and would call her to give her an update as soon as I knew anything.

With coffee cup in hand, I drove out to Northern Pines, the longest drive I have ever taken. I thought that maybe Terry had just had a seizure and with his swimming motions he might have just swum across the lake and was walking around in the woods in a daze. When I arrived at the dirt road that led to the resort, I kept hoping I would see him loping through the woods in his bathing trunks in the morning haze. But of course I didn't. When I arrived at the camps, Marlee met me with a hug and tears. She kept saying it was her fault because she didn't watch him. I shared with her my observation of the seizure he had last Sunday and the fact that I couldn't have saved him even if I was a good swimmer, because of his size.

The divers had not yet arrived. I walked down to the lake and looked at Terry's clothes, still sitting on the beach where he left them. I sniffed his shirt—it smelled like Terry. I walked out onto the floating dock and stood there. The sun was just coming up, illuminating the mist rising off from the lake. I closed my eyes and said a silent prayer asking for help and guidance and strength. When I opened my eyes, I saw three loons swimming abreast of each other down the lake, and as they approached where I was standing, they turned in my direction and formed an arc in front of me, all three of them like posted guards to take care of me. They stayed there until the divers arrived, and I remember feeling an incredible warmth come over me. I decided they were angels sent to look after me in my hour of need.

When the dive team arrived, I discovered that one of the men, Roland Tilton, was someone I had known from South China when I lived out there. What a coincidence. Or was it? They went into the water and started in the shallows along the shore first. Then they asked me if I had any idea where he might be. I said I wasn't with him when he was there last night, but he usually swam between the two docks. I pointed out in the lake, just to the right of the floating platform. While they began their underwater search out in that direction, another man came up and put his arm around me. He was one of the wardens, but not a diver. He said he had a boat, and that when they found the body, they would take it over to the other side of the lake. He wanted me to get into his boat with him to go over there and be ready to identify the body. I said I would do that.

All I could think of was Terry, all alone and cold under the water all night. Within about fifteen minutes, a little yellow float bobbed to the surface, right where I had pointed. The warden told me that meant they had found the body. I felt like I had been kicked in the stomach. I couldn't believe this was happening! Just yesterday, Terry had been walking down the street, full of life!

They pulled Terry up out of the water. When he succumbed, he must have fallen into a slumped position to the bottom of the lake, because when they brought him up, his body was bent over, and when they laid him into the boat, his feet stuck up in the air. He was stiff. He still had his bathing cap, swim goggles, and flippers on.

The warden helped me into his boat, and as I was getting in, I noticed by the tag on his shirt that his name was Albert St. Saviour. Was he an angel? Who has a name like that? He was there for the sole purpose of looking after me. He was kind and gentle and understanding. Clearly, he had done this before. At the other side of the lake, an ambulance was waiting, as well as a couple of early bird reporters and photographers. Albert St. Saviour told me to ignore them and turn my back to them. He escorted me to the boat where Terry's body lay, and I knelt down, touching him gently on the forehead. He was cold and hard, and I said, "Oh, Terry, why did you have to be so stubborn? Now look what you've gone and done! I am going to miss you so much." I caressed his hands for a few minutes and then said it was okay to let them take him away. There would be an autopsy.

After the ambulance took Terry's body away, we went back across the lake and into Marlee's house. I had to make some long-distance phone calls. It was before the days of cell phones (at least for me), so I would have to run up her bill. She didn't care. "Just do what you have to do," she said. "Terry was a good friend of mine. It's the least I can do". But I didn't know who to call or how to get ahold of anyone. Then I remembered that Terry had called his brother Johnny in Nantucket, which meant that the number would have been registered on my phone charges. I called the phone company and explained the situation, and they gave me the number. I called John Crawford in Nantucket, and a French woman answered the phone in very broken English. I asked for John and she said he was not to be disturbed. (I guess he was very important.) I said it was an emergency, and she said he still didn't want to be disturbed. I begged her to go get him, and told her who I was and that it was about his brother Terry. She put the phone down, and after what seemed like an eternity, John very impatiently came to the phone and asked what the emergency was.

I said, "This is Sara I'm Terry's roommate. He has drowned."

John took a minute to respond, and then said, "Oh. Oh my God. We were always afraid we would receive this news someday. Where are you?"

I told him. I said I would be going home and that other family members could call me later at home if they wanted to. Arrangements would have to be made.

After having breakfast with Marlee, although I couldn't eat much, in a daze, I went home. I called Barbara and told her, and just cried and cried. So did she. She then offered to come down and be with me if I needed her to. I said that it would be good if she could come down the next day, because I was going to have to go back to Northern Pines to get Terry's stuff. The sheriff wouldn't let me take it that day for some reason.

Then I called work and said I wouldn't be in for a couple of days. I told them about Terry's death. Then, before I could even think, the phone rang. It was Terry's sister, Liza. She was very nice and said that she and her husband and son would come to Maine right away and help me. Then I received a phone call from Terry's mother, who said, "I have always wondered when this phone call would come. I figured he would die in a car accident. I know he has been very depressed for a long time." She wanted to know how I was doing. What a kind woman. I told her that Terry was happy living with me and that he had found a new zest for life and we were having fun together. He died happy. This seemed to soothe her. I imagine a mother will always feel some kind of guilt, no matter how unrealistic, if one of her children dies before her. In her case, two had now died. Terry's sister had died of cancer several years ago. Only three of her five children were left. I didn't know how to console her. I had never even met her. But she seemed comforted in the knowledge that Terry was happy at the end.

After that, the phone did not stop ringing. All day long, people called, even people from the Quaker Meeting where Terry was a member. They all called with their support and each phone call was incredibly spiritual. These Quakers were so wonderful. I couldn't believe it. At one point, I tried to take a shower, and I answered the phone naked on my way to the bathroom. It was all I could do to go to the bathroom. The family members called several times to make arrangements for the trip here, and for Terry's cremation and memorial service, which would be held at the Quaker Meeting House on Saturday. Then, Terry's blind friend, Bobbi, called. She had learned about it by listening to the evening news on television. What a horrible way to find out her best friend had drowned. She told me that Terry had said he'd found his soul mate. He was talking about me! Soul mate. Yes. That made sense. We were soul mates. I had never used that term before, and I really wasn't sure what it meant. But now I knew. Terry and I were soul mates. So why was he taken away so soon?

Terry's friends from all over Portland called that day. I never got off the phone. As soon as I would hang it up, it would ring again. In a way, all of the phone calls helped to keep me sane. As much as I thought I wanted to be alone, I was in a better place spiritually from all of the support I was receiving. Everyone who called said things that gave me strength and hope. When night finally came, I went into Terry's room, lay on his bed, and hugged his plaid LL Bean nightshirt. It smelled like him, and I went to sleep with it tucked under my nose. I slept only a few hours, with strange water dreams, seeing Terry underwater, not being able to get up to the top, and then realizing I was underwater and also couldn't get to the surface. When I woke up, I wondered if this whole thing had anything to do with all of those underwater dreams I had my whole life. Would I ever know?

The next morning, I had to call Merilyn, whom I had promised to pick up from the hospital. It was her discharge day, and I had to tell her I couldn't help her. Barbara arrived and went out to Northern Pines with me to retrieve Terry's belongings, and then she helped me clean my house for my guests who were due to arrive the next day. I don't know how I would have gotten through it all without Barbara. My angel.

The newspaper carried the story on the front page, with a horrible picture of me sitting next to Terry's body. I was appalled. But there was a full story on the back page about his drowning. The article that appeared immediately above this was about the fact that clamming was returning to the bay after a twenty-year hiatus because of pollution! Terry's dream had come true! All of his work with the Friends of Casco Bay had paid off and ironically, the article appeard right above his drowning story.

Terry's family would be arriving the next day, and I wondered what they would think of me. I wondered if they would even consider me important since Terry had only known me a month. He spent exactly twenty-eight days in my home—one lunar cycle. That seemed significant, but I wasn't sure why. So how would they treat me? Would they blame me for his death? Would they just shove me aside and take his stuff and leave? I was trying to prepare myself for anything.

When Liza and her family arrived, they came up the back way into my apartment, as I had instructed them to. As they came up onto the deck, I noticed that they were all tall like Terry, and each one of them bumped his/her head on the rafters, just like Terry had done. I mentioned this to them as I was greeting them, and it brought a chuckle and broke the ice. They were kind and gentle people, just like Terry. They treated me as though I had been a member of the family. I guess they trusted that Terry had made a sound decision to live with me and the short time span didn't matter.

By the next day, the entire family had arrived, including Terry's mother. They were all staying at the Holiday Inn. They came to my house, sifted through Terry's room and his belongings, and took what they wanted. I think it was good for them to do this, and they spent quite a long time reminiscing and remembering Terry. He had mementos of just about all of his family members somewhere in the room, be it a picture, a crocheted blanket, or a bauble that had been a gift. Terry knew his family loved him; he just felt misunderstood and alone most of the time. And he died alone, as, of course, we all will.

The memorial service was held at the Quaker Meeting House on Saturday. The room was just a bare room with a wooden floor. There was no music and there were chairs placed all around the room three rows deep. After a period of silence, one by one, people began to stand up and speak about their memories of Terry. They talked about his courage, his dignity, his spirit, and his struggle to seek something bigger for himself in spite of his limitations. They spoke about his booming voice and tender spirit, his stubbornness and his tenacity to get a job done.

A man stood up whom I recognized and said that Terry had stayed with his family just prior to moving to my house. I couldn't understand why I recognized him. It didn't dawn on me until after the service, that this was the man whose wife I had cared for at the hospital the night Terry drowned, the man I had talked with at length during that evening. How ironic was this? This wasn't a coincidence. While Terry was drowning, I was caring for the woman with whom he had stayed prior to living with me.

Many people spoke about the work Terry did many years ago in an effort to clean up the pollution in Casco Bay so that clamming could return to this area, and they marveled at the article that had appeared in the paper directly above Terry's story. Other people spoke about his concern for social justice and for resources for homeless and poor people in Cumberland County.

Everyone knew about his seizures and had witnessed them many times. As it turned out, the reason he had been banned from the Quaker Meetings was due to something he had said or done during a seizure, which is why he denied ever having said it. It saddens me that some people have so little compassion.

People read poems they had written for Terry, and many folks had hilarious tales to tell about their escapades with him. But everyone agreed, he could be a stinker when he wanted to! One friend summed him up nicely, I thought, with a quote (he couldn't remember the source): "The reasonable man adjusts to the world around him and finds ways to make things work out okay. The unreasonable man fights against those things that don't seem to fit with him and gets people upset around him. Therefore, all progress relies on the unreasonable men." That was Terry, he said. He didn't know how to just accept those things that didn't work, and that's what made progress. Then he went on to say that Terry was a person with two sides—the bristly side and the sweet guy underneath.

When the service was over, there wasn't a dry eye in the place. And it was as though Terry was dancing around in the center of the room, enjoying every minute of this. We had all brought his spirit into the room. It was incredibly powerful.

Following the service, I was invited with his family to go out on a boat into the Casco Bay and throw Terry's ashes into the ocean. It was a wonderful experience. Putting your hands into those ashes, which felt more like sand, or ground bones, was real—it was solid—it gave truth to his death and allowed for closure. As I spread a handful of his ashes into the sea, I said, "Now, Terry, you can swim forever."

The day of the memorial service was also a big celebratory day in Portland. A new bridge had just opened across the Bay, and the city was abuzz with thousands of people participating in the festivities. Parking was impossible, and we had parked our cars in a tow-away zone. So, when we came back from our boat trip, the cars were gone. We had to pay a lot of money to get them out (Terry's brothers paid for my car!). His family all agreed that it was Terry's last message to them—that it was something he would have done, and he was laughing at all of us right now!

When all was said and done, and the family went back to their respective homes, I felt more alone than I ever had in my life. The grief was more than I could have ever imagined. It felt like I had been kicked in the stomach, and I had crying binges that just wouldn't let up. I played the CDs that I had listened to with Terry, and began to remember the nonstop talking, his need to tell me as much about himself as he could in the time available. Did he know he was going to die?

I walked down on the shore at night, and remembered the nights we walked when he had to tell me all about the water treatment systems in Portland, which I hadn't wanted to listen to. Now I understood. He needed to tell me. Why didn't I listen?

The people at Mercy sent me a plant called a Chinese Evergreen, with one lone white cut rose sticking up in the center. I understood the symbolism and deeply appreciated that they cared so much. Maybe I had underestimated them.

In the weeks that followed, I indulged myself in the grieving process, and I think I wore Barbara out completely. I would call her at all hours of the day or night and ask questions she couldn't answer, while sobbing. I'm surprised she didn't tell me to suck it up and move on. But she understood, and she was kind and patient with me, as always. She knew grief, and she would know grief again in her life. I only hoped I could be the shoulder for her that she had been for me.

The University of Southern Maine posthumously gave Terry his master's degree in public policy. He hadn't quite finished his thesis work, but I had taken his computer discs to them, and they printed and bound the work. In October, I took it to New York and gave it to Liza. They invited me to stay a couple of days at their lovely home in Saratoga Springs, and it was a good visit. Liza was still grappling with Terry's death, and we shared tears on more than one occasion.

I tried to pick up my life where I had left off. But I felt more like Dorothy in *The Wizard of Oz*, and I couldn't seem to make sense of anything. There had been so many connections between myself and Terry that continued to present themselves to me. I would take care of patients at the hospital who had worked with Terry. Everywhere I went, there were more connections. It all made me wonder why it all happened. I remembered the statement that Barbara had made, that "I was being prepared for something." She was right. But what was I being prepared for? I still didn't understand. The question haunted me day and night. Although I felt spiritually enlightened to a degree, I still had no understanding of what it all meant or where I should go from there. Would I be the next person to die?

Somewhere in this period of time, I can't honestly say why, I experienced my first and only desire to drink again. Until this point in my life, drinking had never even crossed my mind. But one day a couple of months after Terry's death, I convinced myself I could be like everyone else and have a glass of wine. I went out and bought a bottle of white wine. I dusted off a wineglass and poured myself some wine. I took it into my living room and sat down, looking at the glass of wine. I'm not really sure why I was doing this—I was actually coming out of the grief and depression. But, somehow, I thought I could drink safely and just move on to a new path in my life, that maybe I wasn't an alcoholic anymore.

I didn't drink it. I did what I have always told my clients and other alcoholics to do—I thought it through. Where would it take me? Would I have a second and then a third glass? How would it make me feel? I remembered the last time I drank, how awful I felt. Would I still feel the same? Would my personality change? Would I drive, and take the risk of getting an OUI? How would it affect my job and my nursing career? Would I be able to stop? I stared at that glass for a long time and then poured it, along with the contents of the bottle, down the kitchen drain. That evening, I went to an AA meeting and took a deep sigh of relief. I was, and still am, an alcoholic. It's called alcoholism, not alcoholwasm. I will always have the disease of alcoholism. But, as long as I don't have that first drink, I can live a wonderful, healthy life; I can drink anything else I want; and I can accomplish anything I want to accomplish.

I decided I had to pick up my life where I left off—wherever that was. I went back to what was natural and comfortable for me. I played my guitar. I continued to work on the song I had started when Terry had first moved inI began to see how the words seemed to fit my relationship with Terry.

I sang it over and over and learned the difficult chords on the guitar until my fingers bled. I would sing it before I went to bed and when I got up in the morning. I would sing it in the car on my way home from work.

When winter came, I saw all the snow and felt the cold, and said out loud, "Terry, your knees wouldn't have been able to tolerate this cold and snow. It's a good thing you aren't here." I talked to him all the time, and I felt his presence with me a lot. I became obsessed with the idea that I would be the next to die, that he was just waiting for me to join him. Geez, I was going nuts! This had to stop.

CHAPTER 25

laying tracks

I needed to find some answers, so, silly as it seemed, I sought out a psychic, a woman whom several of my friends spoke highly of. I had a two-hour session with her, which I recorded. It was all fascinating. But what stood out for me more than anything was this: she said that my entire life had been a struggle - like driving a train, and always having to stop and get out and lay more tracks in front of me, and then move on. Stop, get out, lay tracks, get back in, and move on. She said that now the tracks are laid. I don't have to do that anymore. I have a direction, and I can just drive the train on the tracks.

This was how I had always felt. Life always seemed like so much work, laying down tracks so I could continue on. I don't know if psychics really know but she said the right thing to help me get on my way. Maybe I wouldn't have to struggle so much anymore. What did Terry have to do with this? I still wasn't sure. But one thing was for sure, it wasn't time for me to die. And through my depression and tears, I realized that I was alive! I wasn't dead! I needed to go live! I knew I had better do something about it.

So, maybe it was time to date again. Would it be a woman or a man? Scared and apprehensive, I looked in the personal ads in the paper for both. The ad I responded to was this:

"LAUGHTER NOT LONELINESS to share. Gentle, playful, progressive man, 46, loves: Thai food, The Movies on Exchange Street, sailing by moonlight, xc-skiing, snowshoeing, time with friends, the arts, more? Seeks friend, partner? (38-52). UB introspective, independent and alive."

"Alive!" That word caught my eye. "I am alive," I said aloud. I realized I had been so preoccupied with the possibility of my own death that the word *alive* just woke me up.

His name was David. We met on a beach (the same beach I spent the night on) and walked in the snow with his dog, Nellie. David was kind, gentle, smart, short, and handsome! He was in a good place to start a new relationship. I told him about the situation with Terry as well as my recent experiences with my sexuality. Those things didn't make him flinch or run away, so there was hope for a future! I told him about my sobriety, and he, too, had stopped drinking a few years before.

Shortly after we began dating, I celebrated my fiftieth birthday. I decided that I would draw a line in the sand and proclaim that from that day forward, I would be happy. My happiness, or lack thereof, would be my responsibility, and it would not be credited or blamed on anyone or anything else. I realized that I had the choice to be happy, to heal, and continue to grow for the rest of my life, and that I wanted to live for a very long time. Suicidal thinking was no longer an option.

David and I dated for a couple of years, and the relationship was tumultuous and painful at times. I still didn't know how to be in a healthy relationship, nor did he. We had to work through a lot of issues. But there was never any doubt in my mind about how much I loved him, and that he loved me. So, after actually breaking up twice, we have made it to a better place. We were married on April 22, Earth Day, in 2001, out in the woods wearing our LL Bean boots. We purchased a little bungalow near the ocean, we have a dog and two cats, and we grow closer and more in love with the passing of each day. I am here to say that it is possible to have two soul mates in your life. David is my soul mate, and life is good.

CHAPTER 26

along the path

The experiences I lived through in my childhood and early adulthood caused me deep injuries. Research has proven that physical and sexual abuse and other life-threatening trauma during childhood can bring about changes in brain chemistry. It is also believed that these assaults are stored as memories in the body parts affected. Additionally, the spirit is damaged, and in some cases destroyed. I recently read that research scientists in Switzerland have proven that "out of body" experiences, such as my experiences of flying during the sexual assaults, happen to a lot of people, and they are caused by an interruption in brain chemistry. In the laboratory, they have stimulated certain parts of the human brain and the patients have reported various "out of body" experiences during this procedure. Learning this affirms my core belief that the mind, body, and spirit are interconnected. The healing must therefore encompass mind, body, and spirit.

Most health-care professionals do not realize that, in many cases, physical ailments and chronic pain originate from childhood trauma, from alterations in brain chemistry, or from memories stored in body parts, and they treat with pain medications or surgery. I have worked with several patients who have become addicted to the pain medication, and now they have a whole set of new problems, and are further away from dealing with their injuries than ever. As a nurse, I realize we must be able to assess the whole person and take a look at his or her past in order to prescribe a cure. Healing is a process, not an event, and it must come from within. I believe that to properly address these problems, the person must be willing and able to do the difficult work necessary for healing the injuries of the past. I am aware that I could have ended up in a mental institution for my entire life. Many people in mental institutions have similar stories to mine. I am lucky to have made it out of hell and back into sanity. But, my path was my own individual journey, and although some of my healing processes would work for some people, I do not intend for anyone to think that this is "the way" to healing. There are many new treatments available today to address issues of childhood trauma, in addition to the ones I received, such as EMDR, DBT, Therapeutic Touch, therapeutic support groups, and individual therapy with a compassionate professional, to name a few. There are also several residential treatment programs around the U.S. that include family members and last for weeks and months—as long as it takes.

I do believe, however, there are some universal truths that can apply to all of us in one way or another. These are the lessons I have learned along my path and share with you now.

I have a photograph I took about twenty years ago of a path leading through some ferns and on into the woods. You cannot see exactly where the path goes; it just gets darker as it gets into the woods. When I shot that photo, it was because at that moment, while hiking through the mountains in Vermont, I saw my own message in that picture. My journey is like following a path through the woods. Sometimes the way is clear and easy to follow; other times the path is dark and you can't tell which way to turn. The trail isn't always well marked and it is easy to take a wrong turn. But if I just stop and don't go any farther, because I have no idea which way to go, I will never get anywhere. I have to keep putting one foot in front of the other, with faith that the path will soon reveal itself. If I make a mistake, I can choose another way. But I must keep moving, even if I fall down, and even if I'm frightened.

As I am getting older, I am beginning to get just an inkling of what people refer to as "wisdom." It is something that can only come with time and experience—and healing. As I look back over the last thirty years, I realize that my healing did not come from just having treatment or therapy. It was *living* and following my dreams that enabled me to heal. I hear people tell me, "I can't do that because I'm not healed yet—I have too much pain," or, "I'm too depressed," or, "I'm afraid." What I have learned is that you must follow your dreams—set goals and go about the business of reaching those goals, one step at a time. It is in this journey that the healing occurs. During this journey, you can reach out for whatever help you need. You cannot heal in a vacuum. If you have a broken leg and you are put in a cast, the leg is immobilized for a short time. Then, when the cast is taken off, you must walk on the leg in order for it to heal. In fact, it won't heal if you *don't* walk on it. You must learn to embrace the pain instead of recoiling from it. Your emotional and spiritual healing works the same way. It is a kind of serendipity. Healing is what happens on your way to finding something else! For me it has been marching through paralyzing fear. I developed a mantra that I still use today: "I can function while being afraid." We can let fear stop us—we actually become afraid of the fear itself and it stops us in our tracks, impeding any and all progress. I have learned the difference between rational and irrational fear. Rational fear will get you out of a burning house! Irrational fear will keep you from interviewing for that perfect job.

And what about my old friend, suicide? I said good-bye to her once and for all. She's gone, like someone who died. I will not give myself the option to revisit the idea of suicide. For me, it is no longer the answer. My sister Joyce took her own life eight years ago with an overdose of heroin. Her life was so tortured with mental illness and chemical dependency, she felt she had no other choice. She was so little when our mother died, I don't think she ever had a chance at finding peace for herself. I can only hope that she has found peace now, in death. It was Ernest Hemimgway who said "The world breaks everyone, and afterward, some are strong at the broken places." He, however, took his own life.

I now believe that Terry's death was a planned suicide. It took me a few years to come to this conclusion. I think he knew that if he swam long enough, he would have a seizure. Perhaps he wasn't clearly conscious of it, but I think this is what happened. On the day he died, he was fifty-two, the age of his father's suicide. He would have turned fifty-three in a few weeks. That morning, he sat at my kitchen table, pounded his fist, and yelled, "Suicide is the ultimate 'fuck you' to anyone you leave behind!" I'm not sure who he was saying "fuck you" to—perhaps his father. But I felt the sting of it.

I think Terry and I were angels for each other. He was sent into my life so that he would not be alone in his last days. And he was sent to me to teach me many lessons, one of which was about suicide—that it is not the answer. Life is the answer. I feel so honored to have been chosen to walk through Terry's last days with him. I don't know how or why I was chosen, but Terry changed my life forever, and I will never forget my experiences with him.

I believe there are angels everywhere—for everyone. The problem is, most of us simply don't look up and see them. But they're everywhere, all the time. They take on many forms, like the loons at the lake, and the man at Eastern Maine Medical Center who was leaving treatment so I could ultimately have a bed. They are women with white hair; they are children with innocent eyes reaching out for love. They are here to teach us about life—the meaning of life—which is to love and to be loved. It's that simple! Angels are everywhere.

I learned the lesson about love thirty years ago in my group with Barbara, when she told me she loved me. It was in the process of writing this book that I began to make the mental connections in my life, connections that all stemmed from love. Everyone needs to love and be loved. I see the world held together by love, not gravity. I see a thread of love woven like an invisible basket surrounding the world. All of us who receive and give love and compassion are the woven reeds in the basket. Together, we hold the world together. And, like it or not, those people who do not believe or do not have or give love, get caught up in the weave.

Probably the most important lesson I have learned is that I have choices. We all have choices, all of the time no matter what is going on. If you're strung up by your earlobes in a prison cell, you still have choices, choices about your attitude, your ability to stay calm and seek spiritual guidance. You have choices about how you treat others. And you have choices about whether or not to let your emotions rule your life. Now, this came to me after a lot of work and pain and tears. I had no idea that my intellectual brain could take over and make sound decisions instead of my emotions getting me into trouble time and again. It is in making choices that we let go of someone else making choices for us. We stop being the "victim" and take charge. I made the choice not to let my father continue to molest me once I learned the word incest and realized that it was not an okay thing. I also made the choice to never let anyone abuse me again. It took many years for me to fully realize how to carry out that choice.

Even though my emotional, spiritual, and physical pain were initially caused by my father and other perpetrators of my childhood abuse, the pain was constantly triggered in my adult life as I tried to find my path. However, when I found a path of healing, I took ownership of my pain, I embraced it, and I began the healing process from inside. My peace began when I let go of blame and practiced forgiveness.

When we blame others for our pain, we maintain our victim role and cannot get out of it. We must take that leap and take ownership of our pain, learn to embrace it and live with it. In this process we then can make the choices to begin a healing process and get on with our lives.

Today, my pain or suffering isn't because of someone else. It is mine to deal with. If I give the power over to someone else, I am, once again, a victim. And I no longer want to be a victim of anyone or anything. It took a lot of hard work of trial and error with many loving, forgiving people for me to reach this conclusion.

We always have choices.

My life has truly come full circle. It is a good life. I have a sense of inner peace, and I truly can say I have that one unit of worth that I was born with. I have made peace with my family, and they with me. My family is now extremely important to me, and I treasure each and every member. We all need to receive and give forgiveness. It has to start with our family. We share the same genes and blood. We are connected to them in a more powerful way than with anyone else on earth. We must learn to set aside the anger and hurt and disappointments and learn to love each other. Peace should start at home.

I must emphasize here, though, that if you are being victimized by a perpetrator, it is *not your fault.* But you can and must find the strength to get away from anyone who is hurting you. You have the ability to make new choices. You must reach out to get help from people you can trust to have your best interests in mind. Getting to the point of forgiveness takes a long time. And to forgive does not mean saying everything is okay. Never! But it is letting go of the blame and anger that is toxic to your very being. It is also getting away from the person or persons who are hurting you. The choice to get away is yours and no one else's.

I can say that I am lucky in that my father has made amends to me, and he is not the mean, violent tyrant he once was. This does not happen often. I got away from him a long time ago, and I didn't have anything to do with him for a very long time. Had he not changed, I would still stay away from him. I never saw my uncle again. He died many years ago. I do not believe reconciliation would have been possible with him.

I don't want anyone who reads this book to think that you must allow your perpetrator to get away with what they did, blame yourself for your pain, or continue on with the abuse. You must get away from the abuse and protect yourself. Only then can you make changes.

My sister and I brought our parents to Maine to live out their last few years. It has been a healing process for all of us. My sister and I were their guardians. We have made a pact that our family, no matter how dysfunctional, is still our family. We have come to cherish the concept of family, and we are trying to teach this to our children and grandchildren. They will never have to live without the knowledge that they are loved. They will never be abandoned. They will never be abused. We have changed the course of our family. And, hopefully, our future generations will never have to experience what we went through.

Self-forgiveness is where I am still a work in progress. I have had a difficult time forgiving myself for the way I raised my daughter and for things I did while I was drinking. I ask for help all the time, and slowly I am able to forgive myself, one action at a time. I know this is something I must do. It is all part of my ongoing journey.

My daughter is an adult and is finding her own way in life and doing well, despite the way I raised her. When I apologized to her for my behavior and my treatment of her during her childhood, her response was, "What's the matter, didn't I come out okay?" Just another example of human beings' resiliency and ability to heal.

Scientific research has been conducted on the power of prayer and has shown positive results, much to the surprise of many scientists. Not to me. I recall once early in my sobriety when I was talking to another recovering person about something that was of great concern to me. He said, "Well, have you prayed about it?" I answered, "yes." He said, "Well then, help is on the way!" It was like if you have a medical emergency and you call 911. When you hang up the phone, you know help is on the way, and you can get back to the matters at hand. You won't know the outcome, but you know help is on the way. That is what prayer does for me. And help always does come, sometimes in ways I would have never imagined. I have seen the results of prayer in the form of prayer chains or prayer groups. It can happen on the phone, over the internet, by letter, or in church. But prayer is powerful. Prayer is exercising faith in the possibility of miracles. It is also maintaining our connection with God and with everyone else on earth.

We all breathe the same air, and we all use the same water at one time or another. We shed our skin and grow new skin. It goes into the earth, and everything starts over. We are all connected. People who do not have love in their lives do not feel connection, and it is our responsibility to share the love that will bring them in. All living things are connected, and there is a powerful energy that is part of that connection. I choose to believe that my higher power, which I call God, is that power. His power is in all living things. This is the power of prayer.

I find it so important to laugh, to be able to laugh at myself. Physiologically, laughing triggers neurons in the brain that stimulate the immune system. Laughter takes many less muscles than frowning. Laughter helps to reduce the effects of stress. People who laugh have lower blood pressure, sleep better, and are healthier overall. Laughter is necessary just to get through the day. I used to fake laughter. Today, it is real.

Physical exercise—such as walking, jogging, bicycling, kayaking, or practicing yoga—is extremely important to overall good health. When you exercise, your heart rate increases, sending oxygen-rich blood to the brain. It also works the muscles, opening the calcium channels, increasing blood circulation, and improving overall fitness. It is just as beneficial to mental and spiritual health. I practiced yoga and jogged five days a week while attending nursing school. I don't think I could have gotten through that time without exercise. I always feel better mentally after a good workout. If you aren't physically able to get out and do these things, even just regular stretching can be beneficial.

As of the completion of this book, I have been sober for thirty years, one day at a time. I am working in the community as a hospice nurse, helping people to have the best life they can, even up until death. Many of the people I work with have stories like mine. If for no other reason, I believe I have been put in their path to be a calm presence—a peace messenger. Perhaps I can impact someone else's journey in a positive way. I believe I have something to give back, and maybe, just maybe, I can be an angel for others without them knowing it. (They are angels for me!) I would like to think that I can give my patients a sense of hope and a better quality of life at the end of life, for who knows what lies ahead for them?

I have not been flying much in the last few years. Maybe that is because I now feel safe on the ground. I don't need to escape to the air to be okay. I'm okay just the way I am. I believe I finally have my one unit of worth and I am a whole person.

My husband bought me a piano a few years ago, and I took lessons for a couple of years. The music I make is not by any means perfect, but it soothes my soul and reconnects me to the person I was meant to be. What a beautiful gift of love.

I owe a debt of gratitude to the many, many people—my angels— who have helped me over the years. The best way I know to pay them back is to help others in their time of need. This is how the thread of love will continue. I would like to think that sharing my story can be a beacon of hope for those people who are still hurting.

Today, I believe that there is nothing on this earth that can beat me. Even if something kills me, it will not beat me. I am no longer afraid of what lies ahead, nor am I afraid to look back at the road I have traveled. I believe that my life will work out the way it is supposed to. Each day I make a choice to be happy—and I am. I am no longer afraid to die, but I'm not quite ready to die. I want to live to see another day. To the best of my ability, I try to live each day as though it is my last, because I never know when that proverbial bus will come along and run me over. And I want my time on earth—in this life—to have been spent well so that, when I die, or if I know I am ready to die, I will have no regrets.

"The wounded oyster mends
its broken shell with a pearl."
—Ralph Waldo Emerson

CHAPTER 27

conversation with my father

June 11, 2006

*H*aving taken my dad out to lunch for his birthday, we are now sitting on a patio at the assisted living facility where he resides. Lighting up a cigarette, he says to me, "Did you know that you're named after your great-aunt Sara Loftus? She lived in Ashtabula over on the east side."

"Yeah, I knew I was named after her, but I didn't know she was on your mother's side of the family. I thought she was your dad's aunt. Was she related to your uncle Ed?"

"Yes, she was Uncle Ed's sister. You know, back about twenty-five years ago, I rode my Honda Gold Wing out to California where Uncle Ed's family lived. It took awhile, but I found him. He was living like a hermit in an old, abandoned gas station. He was crazy as a hoot owl. He didn't know who I was. But he invited me in and let me stay for a while. I felt real bad seeing him like that. I'll never forget that trip."

"When did they move out to California?"

"Well, they all lived out in Jefferson when I was a kid. They moved out to California in the forties sometime."

Something in my dad's face changed then, and, looking off in the distance, in a childlike voice, he started talking.

"I remember when I was about eight years old, my mother left my dad and took my sister, Lola, my brother, Bob, and me to live with Uncle Ed out in Jefferson."

"Why did your mother take you away from your father?"

After a long silence, he said, "Because he was molesting me." Tears welled up in his eyes, and his lip quivered. He looked into my eyes and told me the story.

"It started before I can even remember. I didn't know anything different until my mom told me not to let him do it to me anymore. I know I didn't like it much. When we were staying at Uncle Ed's house, my dad came to visit one day. He was sitting in a rocking chair in the living room visiting with my brother and me. Uncle Ed walked into the room and saw my dad and just let loose on him! He hit him in the face several times, until he bled from the mouth and nose, and then dragged him out of the chair, kicked him in the stomach and the back, slammed him in the head until he passed out. Pretty near killed him! I was so scared, I didn't know why my uncle Ed was doing that to my dad—I was just scared for my dad. My mom told me later that it was because he had molested me—my uncle Ed really cared for me. She said she wished he would have just killed him." There were tears running down his face and he looked down at his feet.

With tears in my eyes, I gave him a hug and said, "Dad, you have really been through a lot in your life. It's amazing you're doing so well now. Here it is your eighty-second birthday! I guess we must have strong genes, huh?"

After a long silence, he looked into my eyes and said, "You don't know how much it means to me that you have forgiven me for what I did to you. I'd give anything for it to never have happened. I just don't know how you could forgive me, but I am grateful." Then, looking across the patio where we were sitting outside his room, he said, "Look at those tomato plants. They have blossoms on them! I think I might have a nice crop."

And life goes on, one day at a time.
Love.
Life is love and passion.

In the end, if our earth is to be saved, it will be due to everyone learning to love and have passion for life.

> "Peace is a daily, weekly, monthly process,
> gradually changing opinions,
> slowly eroding old barriers,
> quietly building new structures.
> And, however undramatic the pursuit of peace,
> the pursuit must go on."
> —John F. Kennedy

EPILOGUE

My father passed away in August 2009, with my sister Donna and myself at his bedside. We spent about forty-eight hours sitting vigil with him, and during that time, we talked about our childhood. Because I now could filter out the bad memories, we had the opportunity to laugh out loud about things that occurred and stories we remembered. Because I know that the sense of hearing is the last thing you lose when you are dying, I assume that he heard us laughing. What a nice way for our father to pass on to his next life—listening to his daughters laughing!

My father had always walked around with this grim expression on his face—as though he had the weight of the world on his shoulders. I imagine he had many unresolved conflicts going on inside his head. He never laughed unless he was under the influence of alcohol. Even at the end of his life, he couldn't laugh much. However, after he died, as I was driving home, this wonderful image appeared before me. It was an image of my father, a younger man, walking away. He was wearing a khaki jacket and a hat. His step was light and relaxed. With a big smile, he turned to wave at me. I spoke out loud as I was driving, "Oh, Dad, you made it. You got that awful weight off from your shoulders!"

That is the image I will always keep of my dad. After all we both had been through, I had no more anger or hate in my heart for him. I had found a new place in my heart from which to love him—not as my "daddy" but as "Dad". What happened between me and him took a huge chunk out of him, as well. He never forgave himself for it, and he couldn't believe that I could forgive him. He also believed that if there was a God, God would not forgive him. We had many conversations about this before he died. I hope that the image I experienced after his death meant that he had found forgiveness and peace and healing in his next life.

My sister and I traveled back to Ohio, held a grave-side military service and buried our father's ashes next to our mother. I was quite surprised to see dozens of people attend, some whom I didn't remember, many from the C.E.I., where he worked, who came and told stories about him. A man who had been his supervisor for many years told a story about a homeless family—a woman and her husband and two children—that Dad happened upon while out driving the big utility truck. He brought them home, fed them dinner with us, paid them for doing some chores around the house and let them stay overnight. I remembered those people coming, but I had no idea that they were homeless. There were other stories about thoughtful, kind things he had done for people. This wasn't the Dad I remembered from my childhood and I was pleasantly surprised. However, I do believe that we are all born an "essence child" —with a good soul and a bright spirit – and each of us with our one unit of worth. He had a good soul, even if he no longer had a bright spirit. Deep down, he was a good person whose spirit had been injured— and he had his one unit of worth.

The author is very interested in receiving comments and questions and will try to answer all sincere e-mails.
Please contact her at:
flightintosanity@yahoo.com
or
visit her on Facebook.

www.ingramcontent.com/pod-product-compliance
Lightning Source LLC
La Vergne TN
LVHW011326080426
835513LV00006B/208